BEGINNING TEACHING

Anne D. Cockburn is the Early Years Course Director in the School of Education at the University of East Anglia. She studied psychology at the University of St Andrews and trained as a primary teacher in Edinburgh. Since then she has worked as a teacher and researcher north and south of the border.

Cathy Whalen has long experience of teaching young children and has spent the last three years working with reception classes 4–5-year-old. She is now the headteacher of a first school in Norwich.

Vivienne Gray is an early years practitioner with over twenty years' experience. She has just returned to the classroom following a secondment as visiting tutor to the School of Education, University of East Anglia.

Peter Gibley has been a baker and an actor. He taught British Forces children in Germany before taking over a tiny village first school in Norfolk in 1980. He is now headteacher of a much larger first school in the city of Norwich.

Emma Cameron recently completed her teacher training course at the University of East Anglia and has just taken up her first teaching post in Suffolk.

BEGINNING TEACHING

An Introduction to Early Years Education

ANNE D. COCKBURN

with
Cathy Whalen
Vivienne Gray
Peter Gibley

Illustrations Emma S.P. Cameron

P·C·P
Paul Chapman
Publishing Ltd

Paul Chapman Publishing Ltd
144 Liverpool Road
London
N1 1LA

British Library Cataloguing in Publication Data
Cockburn, Anne D.
  Beginning teaching: an introduction to early years education.
  I. Title
  372.21

  ISBN 1–85396–162–0

Typeset by Inforum Typesetting, Portsmouth
Printed by St Edmundsbury Press, Bury St Edmunds
Bound by W.H. Ware, Clevedon.

A B C D E F G   7 6 5 4 3 2

To Richard with love and thanks

CONTENTS

SECTION III: BECOMING AN EARLY YEARS TEACHER

SECTION IV: THOUGHTS FOR THE FUTURE

ACKNOWLEDGEMENTS

Few books are conceived, researched and written by a single person and this is no exception.

I am particularly grateful to Viv, Cathy, Peter and Emma for their contributions, patience and co-operation.

To the teachers, students and pupils who contributed, my sincere thanks.

I am indebted to Monica Conley, Anne Williamson and Rob Barnes for their assistance in producing the final product.

Thanks are also due to Marianne and Catherine, my publishers, who have smoothed the way by being most supportive and helpful.

And last, but by no means least, many thanks to Richard, my parents, Simone and Anna for being there when needed and disappearing when necessary!

PREFACE

This is a book about educating young children in their early years of schooling. It is intended for those about to begin a teacher-training course and for people contemplating teaching as a career. It is not a highly academic book and, although it has been written for an intelligent audience, it assumes no prior knowledge other than your own experience of life.

The chapters can be read out of order but, for guidance, the book has been divided into four sections:

Section I: On being a young child – Chapters 1 and 2.
Section II: Education and schooling – Chapters 3–6.
Section III: Becoming an early years teacher – Chapter 7.
Section IV: Thoughts for the future – Chapter 8.

Chapters 4, 5 and 6 were written by colleagues who have ongoing and direct experience of the topics concerned. The other chapters are based on my knowledge and experiences as a learner, teacher, researcher and teacher-trainer. Some may argue that I have adopted a very child-centred approach. For this I make no apology. Rather, I would hope that, during the course of their training, readers will reach their own conclusions through study, observation, experience and reflection.

Just as children vary so too do schools and education systems. Throughout I have tried to accommodate readers from all parts of Great Britain, thus, where applicable, there are specific sections on the Scottish, Northern Irish, Welsh and English educational systems.

There is very little technical language in this book. However, different counties – let alone different countries – sometimes use different terms for the various stages of schooling. This book focuses on the first few years of formal education. The data have been gathered from the infant department (4–7 years) of a primary school in Scotland, from Norfolk first (4–8 years) and infant schools (4–7 years) and from students attending an early years course equipping them to teach 4–8-year-olds. Thus the terms 'infant', 'first' and 'early years' have all been used to refer to approximately the same stage of schooling.

This book is about teachers and their pupils in the early years of formal education. The former are almost always female and the latter come in masculine and feminine varieties. Rather than battling with the contortions necessitated by the use of him/her and so on I have tried to avoid being sexist by maintaining the gender of the people actually interviewed. Elsewhere I have generally used the feminine when referring to the teacher and either masculine or feminine terms when focusing on individual children.

SECTION I

ON BEING A YOUNG CHILD

1
CHILDREN

The essence of early childhood is impossible to capture in a few short pages but some excerpts from classroom life may provide glimpses into the fascinatingly rich, and individual, worlds of some young children.

It is 9.30 a.m. on a Tuesday morning in Mrs Jones's class of reception and year 1 children at the Andrew Hilary Infant School. Thirty 4–6-year-olds are busily engaged in a wide range of interesting activities spread across the room. Mrs Lamb, the welfare assistant, and Mr Amos, a parent, are also working in the classroom.

Mrs Jones is currently discussing 'living things' with a small group of five children. Adam, a very vocal 4-year-old, readily volunteers his knowledge of anatomy.

> I don't know how many bones I have got. Well the top one is your skull and your piece in the middle is called your hip. Your tummy piece is called your ribs. In your ribs there is your heart. Your heart pumps up when you breathe. Your food goes down a pipe but I don't know what it's called. Your beautiful lungs help you to breathe. I don't know what they look like but I know they are pretty. My Grandad's aren't because he smokes.

This leads on to a very interesting discussion about the human body during which Mrs Jones poses the question: 'What does it mean to be alive?' Four-year-old Yasmin has little difficulty responding:

> You know things are alive if they grow and things that are not alive don't grow. Yeast is alive because it grows.

After a pause for thought she adds: 'Things that are alive could die.' At this point Helena chips in:

I know a lady who is 100. She died. She wasn't feeling
very well.

Elsewhere in the room Jenny is telling Mr Amos about her recent
holiday:

Mr Amos: Where did you go on holiday?
Jenny: I don't know but it was a long way away.
Mr Amos: How long did it take to get there?
Jenny: Nine or ten minutes.

Close by Susan and Jodie are happily busy with their sums. Susan is working on the addition of 7 and 8 when she turns to Jodie:

Susan: Jodie, can you lend me your fingers?
Jodie: How many do you want?
Susan: Five.

(Jodie holds up her hand and Susan proceeds to count aloud all her own
fingers and then those on Jodie's hand thus arriving at the correct answer of
15.)

Mrs Jones then walks by and Susan explains how she had added 7 and 5
earlier in the day:

Susan: You know how I did it? Well I know six and six is twelve. So
            I added one more to six to make seven and took one away
            from six to make five and then I got twelve.
Mrs Jones: Where did you learn so much about numbers?
Susan: In Australia. I knew how to count ever since I was a baby. I
            learnt my numbers and letters on my computer.

At this point Bobby bounds into the room announcing: 'I'm nearly five
because I'm four and I'm starting school next term!' He is followed by his
mother who has come in to spend some time interviewing the older children as part of her Master's degree. Having settled Bobby happily in a
corner with some building bricks and three of his friends she begins the
following conversation with Ben:

Bobby's Mum (I): What do you do when you get bored at school?
Ben: I get all sloppy and I think: 'This is too easy. I want
                  some hard sums.'
I: Why do all this work?
B: To help us do our maths things because we soon go
                  on to hard things and it helps us to learn our sums
                  and things.

I:	Do you ever see adults doing sums?
B:	No.
I:	So why should children?
B:	To help them learn. Grown ups don't really need to.
I:	Does your Mum ever use mathematics?
B:	Well she does different work from us. She goes to work and she types.
I:	Does your Mum ever use numbers?
B:	Sometimes . . . to count with.
I:	What does she count?
B:	Um . . . nine months ago . . . no, a year ago when we moved to our new house she had to count the pegs to put the curtains up with.
I:	Does she use numbers for anything else?
B:	No.

Bobby's Mum then turns her attention to Justin and asks:

I:	Why do you think you do sums?
J:	That's a hard one! I just like doing them.
I:	Is that why you do them at school do you think?
J:	Yes, I just like doing them.
I:	Do you think your teacher likes doing them?
J:	I don't know.
I:	Why do you think she gives you sums?
J:	Perhaps 'cos she thinks you like doing them.

Meanwhile Mrs Lamb is sitting in the home corner with 6-year-old John who is just recovering from a rather severe temper tantrum. She is about to read him a story when he explains:

Often when you are angry on the outside it's because you are very, very sad on the inside.

Fortunately Mrs Lamb is a welfare assistant of many years' experience who is able to gently encourage John to talk about the worries and anxieties of his difficult home life. She cannot make them disappear but, later in the day, she is relieved to see John laughing with his companions.

Shortly after breaktime Mrs Jones is seen with a new group of children working on 'living things'. Four-year-old Joseph is explaining:

In my body there is lorries that carry things – kind of bubbles. They are white and go round your body.

Out of the blue, Stephen, not wishing to be left out of the conversation, proffers his new-found knowledge:

> The cows get milked on the round bit what carries the milk and the sheep get milked by the tummy.

As Mrs Jones leaves the discussion she is met by 4-year-old Simon who had been asked to draw a variety of shapes on a sheet of paper. He announces: 'I've drawn a nothing' as he presents her with the reverse side of his piece of work. Picking up on the joke, Mrs Jones asks: 'What shape is a nothing?' To which Simon grinningly replies, 'A rectangle.'

Elsewhere in the room Trudie, who has also been working on shapes, reveals her new insight to Mr Amos:

> Trudie: Mr Amos, I know why doors are rectangles.
> Mr Amos: Why is that then?
> Trudie: Because people are rectangles.

Without warning a thunderstorm begins. Some of the children are frightened so Mrs Jones gathers the class around her on the carpet. She explains that there is no need to worry and that the thunderstorm – which, she adds, can also be called a magnetic storm – will be over soon. Earlier in the day Mario and Fred had been playing with some magnets. Hearing the term 'magnetic storm' Mario looks at the rain streaming down outside the window and, clearly puzzled, queries: 'But if it's a magnetic storm shouldn't the rain be going backwards Mrs Jones . . . up towards the sky?'

At this point the bell goes and it is time to line up for assembly. As the children make their way to the hall 6-year-old Frances can be heard very soberly explaining to visiting Bobby: 'We always sing some songs from a lovely book called *Hymns Accident and Modern*'.

Postscript

I have tried to provide a very small slice of events which give a flavour of some young children's thinking without – I hope – proving to be overly sentimental and sickly. All the extracts are genuine but – for the sake of continuity – I have taken the liberty of portraying them as occurring within the same classroom during the course of a morning rather than across many days and classrooms. I have also been generous in the number of adults in the room: certainly, in some cases, you will find the teacher and three others but more often than not a teacher will be the only adult in a classroom.

Further reading

If you would like to read other extracts or books which portray young children I can recommend:

Fynn (1974) *Mister God This is Anna*, Collins, London.

Laing, R. D. (1984) *Conversations with Adam and Natasha*, Pantheon Books, New York.

Paley, V. G. (1981) *Wally's Stories*, Harvard University Press, Cambridge, Mass.

Tizard, B. and Hughes, M. (1984) *Young Children Learning: Talking and Thinking at Home and at School*, Fontana, London.

2
EARLY COMPETENCIES

Introduction

In the past many educationalists held the view that young children were empty vessels which had to be filled. In other words they knew nothing when they came to school and the teacher's job was to fill them up with knowledge. As illustrated in Chapter 1 and as you will discover for yourself, young children are very far from being empty vessels. Granted the majority can neither read nor write when they first enter school but what a wealth of skills and an abundance of learning they bring with them!

In this chapter we shall be exploring some of this capacity and knowledge and I shall explain how you can study these phenomena for yourself. My reason for this examination is straightforward: one of the keys to successful education is knowing how to tap in to each pupil's previous experiences and knowledge and to use it as a springboard to future learning. At this juncture therefore it might be wise for those of you who think of teaching as an easy child-minding job to conserve your energy, put this book aside and go in search of another occupation.

Many readers may find it hard to remember when they were four years old but, when reading this chapter, it may help if you think back to your earliest memories which probably originated during your fourth or fifth year of life.

On arrival at school

Imagine you are entering school for the very first time as a 4-year-old. You are surrounded by lots and lots of people, many of whom are far bigger than you. The noise is tremendous. After walking endlessly you enter a room that is far larger than any you have ever seen. You hardly know a soul and, in a few minutes, you imagine that your mum will be leaving you. You have been looking forward to this day for months and yet, now it is finally upon you, you are absolutely terrified.

Nowadays many children have an opportunity to visit their new school and meet their teacher in the summer term prior to their entry but it requires little imagination to picture the enormity of the reserves a young child has to call upon to see him through his first day at school. Certainly any good teacher will ensure that he has an enjoyable day and that he settles in as quickly as possible with his mother staying until he is ready to say goodbye. Nevertheless, 4-year-olds will encounter, cope with and absorb a huge range of new experiences before their day is through.

The fact that so many children so quickly and readily adapt to the strange new environment of school not only bears great testament to the skill of infant teachers throughout the country: it also demonstrates how very responsible and independent a 4-year-old can be. As you will discover, if highly prized, these qualities can soon be put to further good use by teacher and learner alike.

Now cast your mind back to your early school days. Visualise the games you played over dinner time in the playground. Tag? Skipping? Football? All relatively easy on the face of it but all requiring a high degree of organisation and co-operation: who will be 'it'? Who is allowed to play? Where shall the goal posts go? All these issues are dealt with in a matter of seconds. So much for the fallacies that young children always need to be told what to do and that they are totally unable to co-operate with one another! Admittedly it usually takes patience and skill to harness a child's organisational and co-operative abilities but it is an important step to their independence and will later prove a valuable aid in your management.

Listen in on children's conversations and you will soon appreciate that children as young as 4 and 5 can have very rich and varied vocabularies. Cast your mind back to 4-year-old Adam at the beginning of the first chapter for example: he had no difficulty in graphically explaining his knowledge of the human body. For the majority of reception children it is nonsense to say that their use of language is extremely limited; that does not mean, however, that their fluency will be readily accessible to you as a newcomer into their world. Your attempts at conversation may well be greeted with nods, smiles and monosyllabic yes/no answers. Do not be taken in: as an early years teacher you will discover that your pupils generally have a good knowledge of language and many linguistic skills at their disposal.

Notice too the children's vivid imagination. This is well illustrated by an example reported by Susan Isaacs in 1930:

On one occasion, Phineas (3 years, 10 months) and other children had made a 'ship' in the schoolroom, with an arrangement of tables and chairs. Phineas' part in this was comparatively a passive one, as he was but 'a passenger' on the ship, and was going on with his own pursuits on the voyage, sitting at a table and sewing a canvas bag. Miss D. was with him 'in the ship', and all around them, the crew and the captain carried on the business of the voyage. And when presently a new supply of thread was wanted, and Miss D. said to Phineas, 'Will you get it out of the drawer?', Phineas replied, 'I can't get out of the ship while it's going, can I?' And called out in a stentorian voice to the 'captain', 'Stop the ship! I want to get out!' After some demur, the ship was brought into a 'landing stage', and Phineas got out, secured his thread, and got in again, saying, 'Now, it can go again!'

(Isaacs, 1930, p. 105)

Perhaps Phineas is now a famous inventor exercising his imagination to the full. Or perhaps he is a musician, artist or poet. Or maybe he is just like the majority of us who enjoy escaping from the pressures of this life from time to time to a land of make believe.

A frequent cry of student teachers working in reception classes is: 'They can't sit still for two seconds! I no sooner give them something to do, turn my back for an instant and they are wandering off doing something else!' Certainly finding stimulating tasks for young children can be a real challenge but it is a commonly held fallacy that their concentration span is next to zero: just watch a 4-year-old watching a favourite television programme! Some might argue that being glued to a cartoon is a fairly mindless activity and that it is therefore a poor example of the type of high level concentration required for school but consider the following extract taken from an afternoon's work with a class of reception children.

Miss C. suggested to a group of five 4-year-olds that they might like to build a bridge. She explained that the children must '. . . decide where your bridge is going to go, which way it is going to go in that corner and decide whether you want things to go over it or under it. I don't know what sort of bridge you are going to build: it's entirely up to you.' The children immediately rushed over to the brick corner and quickly separated into two groups with Rebecca, Danielle and Karl in one and Paul and Gemma in the other. Both groups began building bridges. However, within two minutes Rebecca and Danielle were constructing towers instead. These kept falling down much to the girls' amusement. In apparent disgust Karl left them to it and began working independently. Meanwhile Paul and Gemma were attempting to make hump-backed bridges. They appeared to be having difficulty and their success was further hampered when Rebecca and Danielle joined them and began piling bricks on top of their attempts. Nevertheless Paul worked doggedly on with Gemma's help but finally abandoned his seat in the corner when Karl began crawling under – and thus destroying – his sixth attempt at a bridge.

Leaving the others to their tower building, Paul began constructing a bridge several feet away from them. Half a dozen of his efforts collapsed but, by incorporating a nearby table, he showed the beginnings of success. Seeing this Karl joined Paul and together they produced a bridge spanning 6 feet. This attracted several other members of the class and it was not long before model ships were sailing under the construction and plastic people were strolling along it.

In total Paul – a child noted for his extreme lack of concentration – spent over half an hour working on his bridge. When he began the task he was frequently pestered and had numerous failures but nonetheless he persisted and ended up with a piece of work of which he was very proud.

(Cockburn, 1988, p. 9–10)

Another important quality I would like to discuss at this point is that of curiosity. From the moment they are born children are interested in their surrounding world and in establishing their effect on the people and objects around them. It does not take long, for example, for babies to learn what happens when they let out a lusty bellow!

Such deductive reasoning coupled with a real thirst for knowledge is a feature of early childhood which enables children to learn at a far greater rate than at any other period in their lives. Interestingly the same is true of the young of other animal species: if you have had a kitten or a puppy you will know only too well what I mean!

This enthusiasm for knowledge tends to decrease as one gets older but you only need to look into a busy infant classroom to appreciate that the vast majority of pupils still have a tremendous drive and thirst for information. Harness it and your job will become considerably easier and more rewarding. Ignore it and not only will your pupils' education suffer but you will be adding a considerable yoke to your burden. This will be discussed more fully on your training course but, in brief, if you do not challenge a child's lively mind then some other activity almost certainly will!

When discussing children's curiosity I used the term 'deductive reasoning' and I would like to explore that concept a little further before moving on to the next section. Whenever anyone says anything to you or some-

thing happens to you, you automatically interpret it in the light of your previous experience and knowledge. Thus, for example, if I say the word 'beetle' to you, you might conjure up a completely different image to the one I had in mind. I might be thinking of a beloved wreck of an old car while you were picturing a small black insect or a long-haired singer of the sixties! Clearly a bizarre conversation could ensue if I explained that I took my beetle to work each day.

By the time they first arrive at school children have a highly developed capacity to interpret and make deductions from what you say and do. One of the most commonly cited examples of this is when a child who is beginning to master some of the finer intricacies of the English language comes out with words such as 'sheeps' or 'maked'. Such interpretative initiative can create real problems for an inexperienced teacher. Consider the case of the delicious dessert: you begin by having a huge slice of the chocolate gateau and, when offered, you accept some more only to discover that 'more' actually consists of a minute sliver. In other words, 'more' is considerably less than your first helping of gateau. Is it little wonder that children with a hearty appetite confuse 'more' and 'less' in their early mathematics lessons!

Do not be downhearted by such tales though. Certainly your pupils' capacity to interpret meaning can increase the challenge of your work but it can also be put to very good use. Once a child has learnt how to mix blue and yellow, for example, he can go on and use the same technique to create a multitude of new and exciting colours for himself.

To summarise, in only a few pages I have outlined ten important skills that young children possess. Under the right circumstances they can be responsible and independent; they can organise, co-operate and communicate; they can exercise their imaginative skills and powers of concentration and, finally, they have a curiosity and enthusiasm which – coupled with their interpretative skills – can make for interesting and challenging conversations!

At this point I could go on to describe the progression of these various skills from birth through to adolescence. However, rather than compete with numerous others who have written at length about child development (e.g. Bowlby, Brown, Piaget, and Spock), I have decided to focus on how you can learn more about the children in your care by fostering your abilities in observation, communication and analysis. Thus you will develop techniques that are increasingly being demanded of teachers. You will also – I suspect – learn far more about young children than if you confined yourself to reading a book on the subject. (This is one of the principles of learning which will be explored in the next chapter.)

Observing young children

If you are a parent or have had a lot of contact with young children you will already know a great deal about them but have you ever taken the time to really stand back and watch them? Some of you will have I am sure. Nevertheless, as you develop your observational techniques you will be surprised how much there is to learn about your own and others' children.

On starting this section I begin with the sad reflection that – given the suspicions of today's society – it is no longer possible to watch children playing out and about as you risk the possibility of arrest! Of course that is a slight exaggeration but, nevertheless, nowadays any prolonged observation is unlikely to go unnoticed. That is not to say that it is impossible to observe children out in the open: much can be learnt as you simply go for a walk in the park or take a trip to the bank. Notice, for example, how very persuasive young children can become if an ice-cream van comes into sight.

Beaches are very good sites to observe children at play. There you can 'read a book' and watch the hours a child can take to build a sandcastle. How they experiment with different states, materials and shapes and incorporate them into their design: wet sand for the drawbridge, small shells for the windows but larger ones for the doors and so on. The key to such observation is not to be too obvious in your interest for, apart from anything else, as soon as children realise that they are the focus of your attention their behaviour can alter dramatically.

When contemplating observing in classrooms four questions may spring to mind: How? When? Who? What? Briefly the answers are: discreetly, all the time, everyone and anything! More specifically, once you find yourself in a classroom (see Chapter 7 for details on how to organise this) and have explained the purpose of your visit to the teacher, find a spot where you can see the most but intrude the least. If at all possible, try to make yourself less conspicuous by reducing your height to that of the members of the class! This can be done by sitting down (though be sure not to take anyone's seat!) or by squatting. The latter being a skill acquired by many successful infant teachers. Ideally you should be invisible but, this not being possible, do your best to blend into the background. Initially the children and teacher will be aware of your presence but, as they will have plenty of other things on their agendas, they will soon get down to work and ignore you. (One of the biggest compliments ever paid to me as a researcher was that I was 'just like part of the furniture'!) It helps if you have a small notebook so that if a child catches your eye you can simply smile and turn your attention to making some notes. Sometimes a child may ask what you are doing in which case I would tell them briefly and honestly (e.g. 'I am here to learn about your class because I would like to become a teacher').

When should you observe? I would say whenever possible from the moment you enter the school until the moment you leave. Having said that, there are two things you should bear in mind. The first is your stamina for you will discover that active observation (see below) can be extremely tiring and therefore you will need to switch off from time to time. The second is discretion. Every once in a while embarrassing or private events occur in a classroom and it is best if you can absent yourself from them either mentally or – if you can do so unobtrusively – physically. For example a child may become very distressed for some reason or the teacher may be feeling particularly harassed. Tact and diplomacy are the key.

Who should you look at? It is easy to say everyone but it is more realistic to suggest that you observe one or two people at a time. The secret is to focus on the right people at the right time! Incidentally, you might be interested to note that experienced researchers find it hard to observe more than two individuals at a time in any detail but they have an uncanny knack of zoning in on where the action is.

Knowing what to look for is not easy especially if your last experience in a classroom was as a pupil. After all, you probably spent well over ten years in various classrooms and therefore it is not surprising that you are in the habit of seeing things through the eyes of the pupil you were rather than the teacher you hope to become. The important thing is to actively observe for, as Cohen and Manion wrote:

> (if you are) merely content to view passively all that contributes to the flux of classroom life without serious attempt at analysis and explanation, then the experience will be at best valueless and at worst detrimental.

> (1977, p. 107)

I should add that observation without some sort of agenda can be extremely boring! So what should you look for? Certainly you can look for examples of the skills and knowledge described earlier in the chapter. You can also see if you can spot any other unexpected talents the children might have. Look too at what the teacher does and how her pupils respond. For example, as Ward and Rowe (1985) discovered, classrooms are very public places. During their teacher training they observed a group of 4-year-olds working round a dough table. No specific task had been set but the hope was that the children would learn about working with dough and try to make a variety of different objects. When one of the children made a ring and presented it to the teacher, the teacher said: 'How lovely' and put the ring on her finger. As a result all the other children immediately abandoned their artistic and diverse range of creations, made dough rings and presented them to the teacher in the hope that they too would be praised.

There is no doubt that you can learn a tremendous amount through observation but before leaving this section, a word of caution: without confirmatory evidence it can be easy to jump to the wrong conclusions on the basis of a morning's observation. For example, on seeing a child spending most of his time apparently gazing out of the window you might assume that he is a lazy child who is bored by the writing task he has been set. On the contrary he might be a highly motivated child who is very intrigued by the challenge his teacher has set and is working through it in his mind before committing himself to paper.

Whatever you do try to avoid the mistake a student once made on her first visit to a reception class. On seeing the vast majority of children drawing beautiful – and reasonably true to life – seaside scenes she turned her attention to Gemma who was busily scribbling away an orange sea on which her ship could float. The student immediately went up to the child and informed her that the sea was not orange but blue. For the next five minutes Gemma valiantly tried to rub out her efforts and ended up with a hole in the page. On seeing what had happened the class teacher was extremely annoyed: it had taken her months to build Gemma's confidence sufficiently so that she would draw anything let alone an accurate representation of something she had never seen! Had the student stopped to investigate rather than jump to conclusions she would never have made such a devastating error.

Talking to young children

You can pick up a great deal of additional information and insight if you can chat to young children rather than simply observing them. Being able to have genuine conversations with children is a real skill. Some people are naturals but others require quite a bit of training before they master enough skill to have a simple dialogue with a young child – let alone an insightful discussion.

It is difficult to define exactly what makes some people so much better at chatting to children than others but I suspect that it has much to do with genuine interaction and respect for the individual with whom you are having a conversation. Some people never learn to employ the appropriate techniques when talking to their contemporaries let alone their youngers and elders. Not only is this extremely sad but they miss out on the richness of another person's experience and opinions.

Deaf people often become very frustrated when others treat them as slow witted simply because they are hard of hearing. Children too dislike it when they are treated with condescension. I – and I suspect children – find it particularly irritating when I hear adults addressing 5-year-olds in a babyish tone of voice. Young children's vocabulary and syntax may not be as developed as those of an adult (and this must be borne in mind) but, nevertheless, they appreciate an acknowledgement of their role as equals.

One of the most successful ways I have discovered to talk to young children in the classroom environment is to observe them for a while in the manner described above and then approach them and strike up a conversation (if they have not already beaten you to it!). This gives both parties an opportunity to get to know one another from afar and provides you with some valuable ideas with which to begin your chat. For example something like 'You have been working very hard on that beautiful picture' is a good opening line as it shows that you are interested in, and impressed by, what the child has been doing. Occasionally such a comment can be enough to set a child such as 7-year-old Caroline off on a most informative, non-stop monologue:

> Yes, it's a picture of my Mummy. She's 36 and she lives in this house here. And this is my Mummy's boyfriend. He's 40 and he sometimes comes to stay with us at weekends. He's very nice and he always brings me lots of sweets when he comes to stay. And this is my brother, James. He's three and he's a bit of a cry baby and he doesn't like it when I come to school. I like school. My favourite subject is PE. I *hate* school dinners though! Mrs Simpson is my teacher. She's really nice. She said my work was excellent yesterday. That's the first time she's ever said that. What's your name?

At this point it is as well to point out that what you hear from a child should be treated as confidential. Moreover you should bear in mind that sometimes you may be the victim of some rather tall stories! This notwithstanding, if a child does tell you something which appears to be worrying him or which disturbs you, do tell the teacher – or, if it seems more appropriate, the headteacher – explaining the circumstances in which the information was revealed.

The majority of children are not so forthcoming as Caroline but nevertheless, with sensitive handling, they can provide a great deal of insight into their world. This is particularly true when you ask open-ended questions. In other words questions where the answer is not simply 'yes' or 'no' but open to more interesting responses. Rather than asking, 'Do you like school?' for example, you might ask: 'How do you like to spend your time at school?'

Sometimes a child simply may not wish to talk to you. If this happens do not try to cajole him into conversation as this is not only cruel but it is likely to be counterproductive and cause him to tighten up like a clam. Neither should you immediately conclude that you are a failure: even the most experienced teachers sometimes have difficulty striking up conversations with the less communicative members of their class.

Before moving on, pause for a moment and imagine how you feel when you are talking to someone much taller than yourself. It can feel rather imposing. Ponder too the ways that people have intimidated you in the past: perhaps they have shouted or sounded very superior. Perhaps they have 'gone on' at you. Reflect on these situations and consider too those conversations with professionals where you have felt comfortable and re-spected. Try and emulate the good and dismiss the bad and you will have made a good start. If you are unlucky enough to upset a child, try to cheer them up but, failing that, seek advice and assistance from the teacher.

Having made contact with a child there are many directions in which the conversation can go. If you have no particular agenda I suggest you follow the dialogue wherever it leads you as you may end up learning all manner of interesting, unforeseen things. If, on the other hand, you wish to explore a specific topic, it is as well to have some useful questions up your sleeve. I *always* start with questions I know the child I am talking to can answer as this almost invariably gives them a feeling of confidence. Thus, for example, if I am trying to find out more about their mathematical ability I might begin with a question such as: 'If I had two pencils and you had three pencils, how many pencils would that be altogether?' in the knowledge that the child was more than able to solve addition sums involving numbers up to ten.

As a general rule I never tell a child if they have made a mistake as this can deflate their ego and can make them less vocal and more timid in their responses. Rather I praise them for their efforts and encourage them when they attempt something a little unusual and outside the range of their experience. Thus, for example, an interview with Darren – an able child who had been labelled not very able by his teacher – went like this:

Me: You look as if you have been working very hard today. Do you mind if I ask you one or two questions about what you've been doing?

Darren: No.

Me: Thank you. Can you tell me what three minus one is?

Darren: Two.

Me: Very good. What about eight minus two?

Darren:	Six.
Me:	Do you know what kind of sums these are?
Darren:	Subtrack.
Me:	Good guess.

Notice I did not say he was wrong. If I had he might have become hesitant. Moreover there were plenty of other opportunities when his minor error could be rectified. I then went on to ask questions that he would not have encountered in school before:

Me:	If I had twelve pencils and you borrowed four of them, how many would I have left?
Darren:	Eight.
Me:	Now have you got your thinking cap on? [Darren laughed] What is nineteen minus eleven?
Darren:	Eight.
Me:	How did you manage that so quickly?
Darren:	Well I said nineteen take away ten is nine, take away one more is eight.
Me:	You are working ever so hard today! Now here is one you will really have to think about. Let us pretend that I buy ten glasses. Unfortunately I break three of them on the way home so I stop at another shop and buy six more. How many glasses do I now have?
Darren:	Thirteen. Can I try another one like that?

And so the interview continued with Darren successfully completing more and more complicated sums. When he began to make errors however I asked him one or two slightly simpler questions so that I was able to praise him for his efforts and his success.

Sometimes a child's responses fail to reveal the depth of their knowledge and understanding and therefore, if the conversation is relaxed and going smoothly, it is often worth asking one or two more probing questions. The following is a lovely example of this technique which was quoted to me recently. Paul was doing some work on floating and sinking when his teacher presented him with one of those plastic, practice golf balls with holes in it.

Teacher:	If we put this into the water do you think it will float or sink?
Paul:	Sink.
Teacher:	Why?
Paul:	Because the water will go into the holes.

Teacher:	What do you think would happen if I wrapped it in cling-film?
Paul:	What's clingfilm?
Teacher:	It's the stuff you wrap your sandwiches up in.
Paul:	It would sink.

Now the conversation could have ended there with the teacher assuming that Paul did not really understand the concepts of floating and sinking. However it went on:

| Teacher: | Why do you say that? |
| Paul: | Because the weight of the sandwiches would have weighed it down. |

To summarise, when talking to children in an endeavour to learn more about their life in school, start with easy questions, reward effort, ask probing questions if it seems appropriate and everything is going well and – above all – leave the child feeling confident and cheerful.

Finally, having tried one or two interviews for yourself, reflect on how they have gone, refine your techniques by watching others and then have another go!

Key points

- Children arrive at school with an abundance of knowledge and a wealth of invaluable skills.
- You can learn a tremendous amount about children through observation but guard against jumping to unwarranted conclusions.
- Talking to children can also be most informative but treat them with respect and end the discussion with them feeling confident and cheerful about themselves.

Further reading

The works of Margaret Donaldson, Barbara Tizard and Martin Hughes all provide good background follow-up reading on children's early competencies. For example:

Donaldson, M. (1978) *Children's Minds*, Collins, Glasgow

Donaldson, M., Grieve, R. and Pratt, C. (Eds.) (1983) *Early Childhood Development and Education*, Blackwell, Oxford.

Hughes, M. (1986) *Children and Number*, Blackwell, Oxford.

Tizard, B. and Hughes, M. (1984) *Young Children Learning*, Fontana, London.

Another useful introductory text is:

Brown, G. (2nd edition, 1986) *Child Development*, Open Books, Wells.

Many guides on teaching practice have sections on classroom observation as, for example, the book mentioned in the chapter:

Cohen, L. and Manion, L. (1977) *A Guide to Teaching Practice*, Methuen, London.

A book which specifically focuses on the topic is:

Walker, R. and Adelman, C. (1975) *A Guide to Classroom Observation*, Methuen and Co. Ltd, London.

SECTION II

EDUCATION AND SCHOOLING

3

SOME PRINCIPLES OF EARLY CHILDHOOD EDUCATION

Introduction

As with clothing, fashions come and go in education. Talk to any experienced and successful infant teacher however and you will discover that there is a core of educational principles which underlie much of early years education today. They are not new. Indeed many of them were discussed by Ancient Greeks such as Socrates (470–399 BC) and Plato (428–347 BC). Later they were incorporated into the works of Rousseau (1712–78), Pestalozzi (1746–1827) and Froebel (1782–1852). And, more recently, they have influenced the thinking of twentieth century workers such as Dewey (1859–1952), Montessori (1870–1952) and Piaget (1896–1980). In this and subsequent chapters you will note that these educational principles also underlie much of the education in Great Britain today.

Central to the notion of early childhood education is the whole child. If you respect and endeavour to understand children for the human beings that they are then you possess two very important prerequisites for a successful educator. Just what does this imply and what place do these lofty qualities have within the harsh realities of this country's over-stretched, under-financed educational system? In answer to these questions let us begin by examining the purpose of education. We shall then consider some of the emanating principles, many of which will be taken up by Cathy Whalen when describing the day in the life of a first school teacher (see Chapter 4).

The aims of education

Many people have a vested interest in the education of today's youth: politicians who pay the bill; parents who want the best for their children;

employers who want an appropriate workforce and children themselves, to name but a few. (With no effort at all one of my M.A. groups listed no fewer than twelve interested parties.)

Sadly, he who pays the piper – to a large extent – also calls the tune. Thus the seemingly idealistic views of Froebel (1887) who advocated that free self-activity is an essential method in education are unlikely to win many votes at the Treasury: to be financed schools must be seen to fulfil the needs of society. Many – numerous parents and politicians among them – would argue that a sound education comprises the development of literacy and numeracy. Some would go further mourning the loss of systems such as those of the 1870s where education was

> based on mechanical proficiency, the obedience and passivity of the pupil and verbal instruction by the teacher was the rule. Most teachers were instructors and ruled by fear.
>
> (Brown and Precious, 1968, p. 11)

As I shall discuss in more detail however, such a belief is naive and lacks the necessary vision and understanding to produce the efficient workforce of tomorrow. Certainly literacy and numeracy are – and doubtless will be – important but in a rapidly changing technological world they are simply not sufficient. Nor is the ability to turn on, and work, the latest computer. Rather what is required is the ability to be flexible, to determine what is required and to learn, and apply, new skills as the needs of society change and new situations arise. Moreover, not only should the citizens of the future be educated to work, but they should also be educated to play. If a cynical financier should ask why, the response is quite simple: happy, re-laxed people tend to be fitter and generally have the potential to work harder thus costing society less in sickness benefit and creating more wealth. Such a cold, calculating view is unlikely to be popular among early childhood educators (I certainly do not like it!) but in this day and age we must be realistic. More positively, as I shall discuss, such a view need not obstruct or interfere with a teacher's desire to apply some of the fundamental principles of early childhood education.

To conclude, by way of introduction to the next section,

> The best preparation for being a happy and useful man or woman is to live fully as a child.
>
> (The Plowden Report, 1967, vol. I, p. 188)

Respecting young children

As a first school teacher you will be a very powerful influence in your pupils' lives. Ignatius Loyola (1491–1556), founder of the Jesuits, went so far as to say: 'Give me a child until he is seven and I have him for life.' You will be an important role model and much of what you do will affect the children's self-esteem, how they interact with other people and how they view the nature of education and learning. Some of these impressions will stay with them for life. For example, consider any subject you dislike – mathematics, reading aloud, art and music are commonly cited – and think back to your early experiences in the subject. The chances are that at some time in your school career you encountered someone who (i) lacked the ability to teach that subject and (ii) failed to respect you as a whole person (i.e. someone with possible potential but with fears and anxieties too). The earlier the encounter, the more damaging its effect is likely to be. My initial reaction to the idea of reading aloud is still one of panic!

If you genuinely like people you will already have many of the skills which will demonstrate a respect for your pupils. I am simply amazed at how many people do not say 'please' and 'thank you' to their children but it is usually a good indication of how they rate their pupils. Without exception the best students on our training course demonstrate such common courtesies as a normal part of their interactions even if they are feeling under pressure with thirty five-year-olds clamouring round them!

"I felt happy inside when everyone was listening to me."

Taking the point further, as a teacher you will feel under pressure sometimes but it is no excuse to resort to a strategy I once observed a so-called 'efficient' teacher using: she sat at her desk with four 6-year-olds reading to her from different books simultaneously as she was attending to a queue of queries regarding mathematics and writing exercises. Imagine what such 'individual' attention must have done for her pupils' self-image. Certainly it is hard to hear readers but without a doubt I think it is far better for a teacher to sit down with each of her pupils individually two or three times a week and really work together than to catch a word or two from a child every day as she gabbles through her book at the same time as competing with other members of the class. The former child feels valued and learns to appreciate the written word: the latter feels like an inconvenience.

With experience, imagination and awareness you can acquire more of the skills which demonstrate a respect for children and which help create a happy, secure and productive environment. Have you ever considered, for example, why young children all have their own beautifully labelled (rather than numbered) coat pegs at school and why their teachers take the trouble to name a drawer for each of them? It shows that each and every one of the children matter. If every pupil feels that someone cares about them as individuals then they are more likely to relax, and consequently learn, than to fret about where they put their lunch box that morning.

Such regard is likely to extend to other aspects of your world as a pupil. More specifically, if your teacher respects you then she is likely to tell you far more about her aims and objectives – however young you are – than if she does not. She will let you know, for example, what she hopes you will achieve during the course of the day. She will let you know – and may well negotiate on – what she considers to be appropriate and inappropriate behaviour. And when you defy this code of conduct she will be consistent and fair in her reaction. In other words, although she may challenge and provoke you as a learner, through her consistency and respect, she will ensure that the classroom is a predictable and secure environment in which to learn.

Finally, a respect for children acknowledges that each and every one of them is different with their own individual experience of life, abilities and needs. Moreover, these needs are not always the same as those of an older person for young children are not mini-adults. Childhood is an experience in its own right. It can never be recaptured. And if one has any real hope of realising one's full potential as a human being then one must be allowed to be a child in one's formative years. To some – the financial cynics among them – the implications of this (see below) may seem to complicate life unnecessarily. To others the diversity and youth of their pupils present a richness and a challenge rarely found in other careers.

By way of summary and introduction to the next section let us turn to Plowden again:

> The school sets out deliberately to devise the right environment for the children, to allow them to be themselves and to develop in the way and at the pace appropriate to them.
>
> (1967, p. 187)

Young children's learning

There are many theories of learning and numerous volumes in which they are described, discussed and debated. Rather than explore them here however I think it is more valuable to consider some general principles and their relationship with young children's learning.

Recalling the discussion of the financial cynic mentioned above: nowadays there is far less need for the 'factory fodder' of the late nineteenth and early twentieth centuries. Instead we need more people who have initiative, demonstrate responsibility, are flexible and can work co-operatively with others. (It is worth pointing out that the production rate of a famous car manufacturer rose considerably when, rather than assembly lines, small teams became responsible for the making of a car from start to finish.) So what are the implications for schooling?

First and foremost start with the child's knowledge and interests. Then build on what he knows and endeavour to provide him with challenge and success. Such a philosophy runs through the National Curriculum as illustrated in the Non-Statutory Guidelines for Science:

> it is important that we should take a pupil's initial ideas seriously so as to ensure that any change or development of these ideas, and the supporting evidence for them, makes sense and, in this way, become 'owned' by the pupil. . . . Activities must challenge all pupils and, at the same time, provide them all with success at some meaningful level.
>
> (1989, pp. A7 and A9)

Take this book as another example: throughout I have tried to link my discussion to aspects of your life. I have then tried to extend the discussion and, now and again, provide you with thought-provoking reflections and questions. Obviously I am unable to assess and praise you for your labours but, if you are aware of gaining some insight into the nature of early childhood education, then you will no doubt feel some satisfaction and a

sense of achievement. Throughout I have run the risk of your misinterpret-
ing my discussions. These misinterpretations may arise because of ambigu-
ities, or inaccuracies, in my writing or the history and understanding you
bring to your reading. I can do little about that but, as a practising teacher
you, on the other hand, will be able to check on your pupils' understanding.

In the past the school system has often failed to take into account the
need to link old and new knowledge and interests, with two particularly
serious consequences. The first is that, having crammed in numerous,
seemingly unrelated facts for an examination, the pupil rapidly forgets
them. And the second is that an uninterested individual may well build up a
resistance to the subject which could prove difficult to break down. Such a
resistance can have extremely long-term effects as described in books such
as, *How Children Fail* by John Holt (1964) and Laurie Buxton's (1981), *Do
You Panic About Maths?*

The ideas of linking something both to a child's previous knowledge and
to her interests often go together but I vividly remember one occasion
when I was 9 and my teacher began a lesson by accounting for neither.
Thanks to the hand of fate, however, our interest was soon aroused and a
scientific principle was lodged in my head forever. Basically Mrs X was
endeavouring to teach us about forces. Her demonstration included a basin
of water, a jam jar and a piece of cardboard. Filling the jar with water,
sliding the cardboard over the top and inverting it all resulted in an al-
mighty flood: so much for the force of air pressure intended to push the
cardboard onto the jar!

Mrs X's demonstration almost certainly taught everyone in the class
something about forces that day but, even if you had a constant supply of
such dramas, you would soon find that they ceased to have effect. Sadly the
same is true of news documentaries which, for most people, have to become more horrific if they are to continue to have an impact.

Disastrous demonstrations aside, let me now contrast two evening
classes I have attended which illustrate the need to relate to the learner's
knowledge, experience and interests. One was an immediate and long-term
success and the other was an instant, irretrievable fiasco. I enrolled in both
for very similar reasons: I lacked specific knowledge which I felt I ought to
acquire. Both classes comprised males and females of varying intelligence,
interests and skills. Both teachers were males in their late thirties with
considerable teaching experience.

The classes began in a very similar manner: the teachers introduced
themselves and then asked each member of the group to give their names
and very brief accounts of their knowledge and interest in the subject.
There the resemblance ended, for the car maintenance teacher sneered at

the responses of all but the most avid and knowledgeable members of the class and immediately began to teach at a level which only the most advanced members of the class could follow. In contrast, the Italian teacher delighted in our presence and – after some examples – pointed out that we already knew several Italian words: 'pasta', 'ravioli' and 'risotto' to name but a few. Five minutes into the car maintenance session and I was wanting to vanish away in a haze of embarrassment and ignorance. In sharp contrast, five minutes into the Italian lesson and I was beginning to think I could speak like a native! Somehow I managed to survive my one and only session on car maintenance. Even though I knew I was not the weakest member of the class I realised that further lessons were an entire waste of time as the instructor had already planned his course in detail and it was intended for the most knowledgeable – and only the most knowledgeable – amateur car enthusiasts. I suspect even if the class had consisted of people solely like myself it would have made little difference to the content of the course for it appeared that – as far as the teacher was concerned – his actual pupils were irrelevant to him. Six weeks into Italian lessons and I feel confident enough to use my Italian on holiday, find a hotel room, order myself something to eat and drink and even buy some postcards and stamps to send to my family in Scotland. I wrote Scotland deliberately for – unlike the other teacher – Raphelli actually wanted to know about his pupils and throughout he tailored the course to meet our individual needs. Certainly I am not the most fluent in the Italian class but at no time have I been made to feel that I am holding the group up or that I am attempting something far beyond my capabilities.

Finally, another marked contrast between the teachers was that one most definitely taught a series of facts while the other provided opportunities for learning. Sometimes Raphelli did teach us specific points of grammar or vocabulary but he also gave us chances to experiment and make discoveries about the language which would have remained hidden had he been more didactic (i.e. purely instructive) in his approach.

Thus an able, empathetic teacher, early success and subsequent confidence have set me on the road to becoming a reasonably competent Italian speaker but failure, humiliation and a total lack of understanding on the part of another teacher mean that I am unlikely to open a car bonnet again and – in the absence of a miracle – I am never going to become anything approaching a car mechanic. The same is true of young children but the balance between possible success and failure is even more critical bearing in mind that school is likely to be their first encounter with any formal education. As their teacher you have the opportunity to set them on the road to achievement and success or to damn them to humiliation and failure.

To summarise, in this section I have illustrated some of the more important principles of learning: start with the learner; build on what he or she knows; provide challenges and opportunities for learning rather than just instruction and – a crucial point – ensure that the learner experiences satisfaction and success.

Educating young children

How can a teacher possibly educate, let alone assess the knowledge, experience and interests of, a room full of four- and five-year-olds? If you have been with one – let alone thirty – reception (i.e pupils in their first year of school) children you will know that – assuming they are not ill or asleep – they are bursting with energy and enthusiasm. There is simply no humane way (see below) that you can sit them down, give them a paper and pencil test and leave them to get on with it. And yet, by the end of their first year of school, children have acquired a tremendous amount of knowledge and are well on the way to mastering the skills of reading, writing and mathematics. Their teacher must have taught them all in some way but how on earth did she do it?

First let us consider an approach which many would applaud but which, at best, produces very limited results and, at worst, can be inhumane. Basically the policy is to ignore the individuals and treat the class as a 'job lot'. The cynical financier mentioned earlier for example would, no doubt, advocate making even the youngest pupils sit down, and then teaching them all exactly the same things. They would not like it and there would be tears but, through the sheer force of authority the teacher would be able to quell 'any nonsense', induce a 'healthy' sense of fear and respect, drilling the children to a standard of attainment commended by many. The problems created by such a system unfortunately tend to lie hidden and, in some cases, dormant for several years after this formative period. Putting the psychological damage aside (for our financier would not be particularly interested in it) let us consider now the outcomes of such a system.

Almost certainly nearly all the pupils would be able to read, write and complete pages of standard mathematics by the time they left school for fear is an excellent motivator. Research has demonstrated however that they are likely to have little understanding of the material they have been taught even if they do manage to remember it. Thus, when faced with a new situation, they are likely to flounder being unable to apply their knowledge and having very little, if any, idea about how to find the necessary information for themselves. How many of you, for example, were taught that '−' means 'take away' and that you must always take the smaller number from the bigger? How would you cope if you had to explain in a life and death situation that three minus negative nine thousand (i.e. '3 − (− 9,000)') equalled 9,003 assuming, of course, that you could remember the rule which no doubt was learnt hurriedly for an examination that 'two minuses make a plus'. That is a fairly frivolous example but I will wager that the more class-taught and formal your education was, the more likely you are to have difficulty when applying your knowledge to new situations unless you are a naturally adaptable and inventive individual. As the Non-Statutory Guidelines for Mathematics in the National Curriculum point out:

> it is . . . important that pupils learn how to use their mathematical knowledge and skills to tackle a wide variety of problems. For most pupils, the main point of learning mathematics is to be able to use it effectively.
>
> (1989, p. B8)

Again (remember the car maintenance instructor?) it appears that mass − rather than individual − teaching is unsatisfactory for our purposes. So what is appropriate?

In Chapter 2, I discussed how much you can learn from simply watching a child and this is exactly what experienced infant teachers do: they observe their pupils and then plan their work accordingly.

Now clearly a reception teacher cannot just provide her new intake of children with an empty room and hope that they will happily go about doing something which will tell her exactly where to begin their work with her. Rather she must provide opportunities and tasks for them which are likely to engage their interest and attention and note how they respond to the experiences. Obviously she cannot observe all her pupils at one time and therefore in the first few days of the term she will provide a range of activities which, on the basis of her experience and training, she knows will occupy the children profitably. For example she might set a group of four the task of setting the table for 'dinner'. From observing this activity the teacher will soon pick up indications of the children's mathematical knowledge (e.g. who can sort the cutlery? Who can match the knives and forks? Who can count?), which children are fairly extrovert and appear to have a good facility with language and which children seem to work well together. These hunches she can confirm by chatting to the children and setting them other tasks which will focus on particular aspects of their behaviour.

Elsewhere in the room the teacher might have laid out some bricks for a group to play with. This, the cynical financier might argue, would be a total waste of both time and the tax payers' money: on the contrary, play is a highly informative and valuable component of the first school curriculum. Come to that it is an extremely important part of all our lives! This will be explored more fully at the end of the chapter but, suffice it to say, an experienced teacher can learn a tremendous amount about her pupils by observing them as they play.

In another area some children might be experimenting with various musical instruments, and so on.

Returning to the teacher: what can she do with the mass of information that she has accumulated about each of her pupils? Not only will she have discovered that they all know different things and have had different experiences in their lives but it is likely that she will also have observed that they respond differently to different types of learning situation. The same is true for a group of adults: you might be the sort of person who learns some things by observing someone else and understands other things by thinking about them and tackling thought-provoking problems. Your friend, on the other hand, might acquire the same knowledge by engaging in practical work in both cases. Moreover, if you consider your own learning you will appreciate that, if you tackle something new using one approach (e.g. practically) and then adopt another approach (e.g. reading about it) you tend to gain a greater and broader understanding of the topic. For example you might try your hand at fishing and catch very little on your first outing but, after reading about it when you got home, you might be far more successful on your second venture to the river. The same is true of children: each topic can be approached in a variety of different ways each of which can provide additional insight into the focus of your attention. The Non-Statutory Guidelines for the National Curriculum in English recommend that

> pupils should encounter a range of situations, audiences and activities which are designed to develop their competence, precision and confidence in speaking and listening . . .

(1989, p. 13)

Some would argue that ideally, for each child in her class, a teacher should provide an individualised package of activities which would build on the knowledge, interests and experience of that child, take into account that individual's preferred learning styles and meet the needs of society. An exceptionally tall order which would kill even the most dedicated of teachers within the week! Fortunately, while acknowledging the differences, there are also similarities in children's responses and behaviour and it is possible for teachers to make use of these patterns. Thus infant teachers can – and many do – group their pupils so that the tasks each group is given cater in some way for the needs of all the individuals within that group. Thus, for example, an activity might really challenge Josh but prove to be a useful revision for Simon. Both would gain from the experience but, rather than having had to provide thirty individualised tasks, their teacher was able to plan for just six groups bearing in mind the need to amend the work for any child if necessary.

Teachers also need to be aware, however, that their pupils' needs and experience – let alone their interests – are constantly changing. Thus on one day a child may be introduced to finger painting and several days later he may be applying the technique as they learn to develop the more advanced skill of pattern making.

To summarise, to provide the right task to the right child at the right time is no easy task! Take heart, however, for even the most experienced teachers find it hard (i.e. to match work to their pupils' needs, interests and attainments). Just remember that one of the many challenges of teaching is to constantly observe, evaluate and amend accordingly.

One final and important point: to take an analogy, think about how you learnt to ride a bicycle or drive a car. You no doubt focused on one aspect at a time but, in doing so, you could not ignore other aspects without serious consequences! For example, as you were learning to change gear you still had to give some of your attention to the steering. Similarly when learning anything worthwhile you may focus on, say, the mathematical aspect for a time but, in so doing, you cannot completely ignore the language surrounding the situation. Every topic you explore and learn about almost certainly consists of two or more 'school subjects' if you really think about it and in the world beyond school you seldom, if ever, stop to consider: 'Well, now I am thinking about science and now I am thinking about art'. Rather you try to understand what you are working at and, if necessary, you break it down into segments which make sense to you rather than dividing everything into 'school subjects'. Making a cake may well involve mathematics, chemistry, domestic science and language but, when developing your expertise in cookery, you focus on the skills of beating an egg, mixing in the flour and so on. Which brings me to the last basic principle of this section: people do not acquire knowledge and understanding in terms of traditional school subjects but in terms of utility and focus. Hence, as you will discover, many infant schools advocate an integrated curriculum teaching through themes and topics rather than science, art, music and so on.

By way of summary, the most effective teachers are those who are aware of their pupils' ever changing needs. As far as possible they endeavour to provide appropriate tasks for the individual members of their class. Frequently this may entail grouping the children and often it will involve a cross-curricular approach to traditionally accepted 'school subjects'.

The value of play

Earlier in the chapter I mentioned that play has an important role in early years' classrooms and it would be wrong to produce such a book without giving the matter further consideration. More specifically, play serves several fundamental functions. It can prove to be an excellent learning experience because, in building a tower of bricks, a child can learn much about shapes, sizes, number and forces in a stress free situation. Moyles is adamant about this:

> The page of sums can only be right or wrong and, in this instance, 'wrong' means the child is and feels a failure. . . . One of the major features of learning through play must be the opportunity it provides for learning, without threat, from those things which go wrong.

> (1989, p. 28)

Apart from reducing stress the sheer activity involved in such play can be a valuable aid to learning as the old Chinese proverb suggests:

I hear, and I forget;
I see, and I remember;
I do, and I understand

(Nuffield Mathematics Project, 1967, title page)

Play too can ease the transition from home to school for it must be quite a shock for a young person transferring from the informal environment of the first four years of their life to the relative formality and structure of school. And, the easier the transition, the faster a child will relax in school and the quicker she should be able to learn what is on offer, which should satisfy even cynics.

Another important function of play in the early years' classroom is that – like so many other activities – it can give the teacher valuable insights into her pupils' educational and emotional experience, needs and interests.

During the course of your training you will learn more about the value of play but, without going into detail, there are two other benefits accruing from such activity which should not go unmentioned. The first is that, quite simply, play can provide a much needed breathing space among all the new and demanding experiences facing a child at school. If we are honest, we as adults frequently take time out now and again and, as a consequence, usually return to our work feeling fresher and more efficient. How many times have *you* stopped and looked out of the window for a few minutes while reading this chapter for example?

The second point is that play can provide an excellent medium through which children – and adults – can explore and, sometimes, resolve some of the emotional difficulties in their lives. In the early years of schooling such a process can frequently be observed when one of the children has recently been introduced to a newly arrived baby brother or sister. A fascinating book which vividly illustrated the value of play for me was Axline's (1964) true story of Dibs, a severely disturbed little boy who slowly, but surely, began to realise his potential through play therapy.

During the course of your training and future careers, you are likely to come across people who view play in the classroom as nothing but a waste of time. If it occurs at all, they may argue, it should be confined to Friday afternoons when the children are 'generally too tired to do anything useful'. Such an argument is woefully shortsighted for, apart from anything else, its absence is likely to leave gaps in the children's knowledge and understanding. Take the example of a two-teacher primary school I visited several years ago. The infant teacher was most anxious that her pupils should be allowed to play with sand and water in her classroom but the headteacher – who took the junior classes – was adamant: there was to be no play of any kind in the classroom and sand and water were totally out of the question as they were both dirty and messy. He then complained that when the children came to him as juniors they had no conception of capacity and volume!

So again we can see that a principle of infant education – the freedom to play – is not just an idle whim of someone with little else to do: it has a real and important function in the early years of schooling.

Key points

The tradition of early childhood education has evolved several significant principles. These include:

- Start with the child.
- Through observation and discussion assess their knowledge, needs and interests.
- Build on what they know.
- Teach for understanding.
- Provide a variety of learning opportunities including plenty of play and practical work.
- Consider how children learn before assuming a subject-based approach.
- Respect the whole child.

Further reading

The first four books all provide good, accessible introductions to the principles and practice of early education:

Anning, A. (1991) *The First Years at School*, Open University Press, Buckingham.
Bruce, T. (1987) *Early Childhood Education*, Hodder and Stoughton, London.
Chazan, M., Laing, A. and Harper, G. (1987) *Teaching Five- to Eight-Year-Olds*, Blackwell, Oxford.
Davis, R. (1988) *Learning to Teach in the Primary School*, Hodder and Stoughton, London.

Axline's thought-provoking book which I mentioned in this chapter is:

Axline, V.M. (1964) *Dibs: in search of self*, Penguin, London.

Other interesting books on play include:

Manning, K. and Sharp, A. (1977) *Structuring Play in the Early Years at School*, Ward Lock Educational, London.
Moyles, J.R. (1989) *Just Playing?*, Open University Press, Milton Keynes.

There are many books on learning but introductory texts include:

Hill, W.F. (4th ed., 1985) *Learning*, Harper and Row, New York.
Howe, M.J.A. (1984) *Psychology of Learning*, Blackwell, Oxford.
Pollard, A. (1990) *Learning in Primary Schools*, Cassell, London.

And for when the principles of education have not been applied:

Buxton, L. (1981) *Do You Panic About Maths?* Heinemann, London.
Holt, J. (1964) *How Children Fail*, Penguin, Harmondsworth.

4

A DAY IN THE LIFE OF AN INFANT TEACHER

Cathy Whalen

Reception Teacher at Avenue First School

7.30 a.m., Monday morning and I am already calculating my arrival time at school. I choose to arrive early as this allows time to chat with colleagues, prepare the classroom and deal with any unexpected situations which may arise. They invariably do, so my first priority is to organise the classroom activities and prepare the materials the children will need.

I am a reception class teacher at a first school which caters for children from 4 to 8 years of age. I am also the deputy headteacher, so my role and responsibilities extend beyond the classroom to the school as a whole and its local community. This is my fifth year here and I feel happy, settled and eager (some would say too eager) to arrive each day. It is a school which takes children from a mixture of home backgrounds in a stable and supportive community. The ethos within the school itself is welcoming and friendly. A place where the individual is valued, sensitivity and politeness fostered and parents, governors and friends encouraged to take an active part in the daily life of the school. We aim to stimulate the children's curiosity and desire to explore and learn within a secure, exciting and happy environment.

There is so much to do before the children actually arrive. Tables to cover with newspaper ready for art and craft activities, painting equipment to organise and a variety of papers to cut ready for the children to use. The computer has to be set up (it spends the night in the hall where it is covered by a security alarm) and I have to choose an appropriate program for the children. We'll be watching a video story on the TV which fits with our current theme so I need to find the right tape in our resources room and cue in to the story on our playback machine. Once the children arrive there will not be another opportunity even to visit the loo until break time. This is the time to think my own thoughts, run through the activities I have planned for the day and check my notes to ensure that I have all I need.

If the children are to be independent and resourceful within the room then everything they might require needs to be available, well organised and easily accessible. There is a rich bank of resources permanently available for them to use: a wide variety of coloured pencils, lead pencils, assorted felt tipped pens, crayons, sellotape, stapler, scissors, hole punch, junk materials, glue, writing and drawing paper, paper with lines, paper without lines, ready-made books in which they can write and draw their own stories, bits of string and rulers. It is the children's responsibility to choose the materials they might need for whatever they are doing and pots are provided for them to carry their selection to where they will be working in the classroom. It is my responsibility to ensure that the pencils are always sharpened, the glue pots full and as wide a range of materials available as possible. When children have finished using equipment they are expected to return everything to its appropriate place in the resource area. This saves me time and encourages them to grow increasingly selective, resourceful and independent. Even at 4, they are capable of organising themselves this way if they are encouraged to do so. Teaching them how to use this equipment appropriately, economically and efficiently is a major part of their learning when they first enter the reception class. Some children will have had little opportunity to use such a variety of resources prior to starting school. I teach them how to use scissors, the stapler and glue effectively and provide opportunities for them to practise these skills in a variety of situations.

Our current whole-school theme is 'pattern' and many of the learning activities I have planned for the day are related to this. Each table, or area of the classroom, will have a different activity for the children and these will take place simultaneously. The children know that they will be expected to attempt everything at some time during the day and will move from one activity to another. Some activities are more highly structured than others and they range across the whole curriculum. It is not possible to cover everything each day, but over a period of weeks a balance of experiences will be provided. Beyond this, each child's social, emotional and spiritual development must also be catered for. A continuous frustration for a teacher of young children is one of limited time. It is never possible to explore everything as thoroughly as I would like, but the important things to bear in mind are the quality of experiences provided and the potential for learning which they involve. My role is not simply to occupy the children.

Today, there will be a table where the children can mix their own shades of blue using powder paints, palettes and water. I want them to experiment and find out about colour – blue in particular – and paint simple patterns using only shades of blue. They already know how to mix the paint for themselves and we have looked at shades of blue on our clothing and in the classroom. They are aware of pale blues, navy blues, dark blues, greenish blues, turquoise blues and purplish blues. Now I hope they will extend this knowledge and understanding through colour-mixing. It will involve artistic and scientific concepts as well as oral language as they discuss together the results of their experimenting. Quite demanding for 4-year-olds.

Another table I cover with a whole variety of children's picture books from our book corner. Many are stories we have read as a class or shared on a one-to-one basis. Some will be old favourites from home. Other books they have not met before. They are there for the children to browse and read as they please. There will be times throughout the day when I sit with a child or children at this table to share books they have chosen to read.

"If someone has an idea, and someone else has an idea and the person talks about their idea – well, you can learn about their ideas and build up more ideas ...."

The writing box, containing everything they may need to write or make a book, goes in the centre of another table. Several maths games go on to another table. Many of the children have learned on previous occasions how to play these and will either play them with a friend (perhaps explaining how to play) or alone. I encourage them to make up their own rules as well as introducing other possibilities. Many mathematical operations are performed while a game is in progress. These frequently involve recognising number symbols, using dice and counting. The children become familiar with number patterns and use mathematical language as they play. Sometimes I will become involved, participating in the game or asking them about it. From observing and talking with them I can begin to assess their level of understanding and mathematical development. This knowledge is crucial if I am to provide activities that 'match' their particular level of attainment.

The sand tray is a permanent and popular feature of the classroom. At the moment the sand is dry but I will suggest that the children add some water and notice what happens. How is wet sand different from dry sand? What can they find out? Can they make holes in the dry sand? Can they draw some patterns in the sand and some letters from their names?

The 'playpeople', building bricks and construction toys provide potential for imaginative and co-operative play. Some children will talk with each other, plan and play together while others will engage in solitary play alongside them. This kind of activity needs less adult supervision, but is a perfect opportunity to observe children, listen to the language they use and see how they interact together.

It is pointless organising too many activities which will demand a great deal of my active participation or supervision. So I provide a balance of experiences which will allow me time to circulate and slip in and out of involvement. If I have an adult helper (parent, student, playgroup helper), which I frequently do, then I need to talk with them about the activities provided and what the children are expected to achieve and learn. The more adults who can be in the classroom to talk with and listen to the children the better. It relieves the pressure for attention and assistance from me and helps the children to feel that what they are doing is valuable. It is not possible for me to share a story, help each child learn a new skill and play a new game each day. But if I welcome parents into the classroom, the crucial role they have played in their child's education prior to starting school can be extended. They can see what kinds of things children do and understand why.

All day today I have a student with me training to be a nursery nurse. He is a regular helper in the classroom and closely involved with the planning and organisation. Before school we discuss the day's proposed activities together, fully aware that these will inevitably be modified as the day progresses. Flexibility is an essential quality required of anyone working with young children. If we are encouraging children to take responsibility for their own learning then we must be prepared for. and welcome, changes in direction which they initiate. I ask him to start the day with the children at the writing table. Through talking with them he can help them express their ideas, decide what the purpose of their writing is to be, sometimes being their scribe and sometimes encouraging them to experiment with writing themselves. By writing alongside them himself he can demonstrate what is involved in writing and the reasons why we write.

Fifteen minutes before the children arrive and the classroom is nearly ready. I spend some time talking with my colleagues, sharing weekend experiences, and possibly asking to borrow a piece of equipment or a book which I will need for the afternoon session. Prior to school starting, there is always the need to chat with the headteacher about aspects of the day: timetables, visitors to the school, what hymns to play in the assembly and her day's agenda. Time always passes so quickly at this point.

Already I can hear children's voices as they assemble in the playground. School officially starts at 9 a.m. but we encourage parents and other adults who bring the children to share books with them in the classroom for about ten minutes prior to this.

Children and adults begin to trickle into the classroom. It's important that I am there to greet and talk with them and make this part of the day as natural and enjoyable as possible. For some young children and their parents, the point at which they have to say goodbye can be difficult and distressing. I try to be available to distract and involve the children in conversation and establish relationships which can be a temporary substitute. I know the children whose need is the greatest and I watch for their arrival. One little girl, who has only been at school for a few weeks, shadows me around the classroom for most of the morning. In time she will feel sufficiently secure and confident to leave me more frequently. Until that time I accept her need to observe the classroom from my side and to attend school for the mornings only. It is school policy that 4-year-olds should not attend full time until they are ready to do so.

As more parents leave, I settle myself in the carpeted book corner, the area where we gather as a class, and proceed to read some stories to the children who are already there and waiting. Gradually, more and more children join us and the last adult leaves the classroom.

Registration is an opportunity for some fun and thought. As I've just been reading a story about a tiger, I suggest an animal register. There is great excitement. Each child has to think of an animal and substitute it for my surname as I call their names. I respond with the sound that the animal makes (if indeed it does). 'Luke?', 'Yes, Mrs Elephant'; 'Sam?', 'Yes, Mrs Mouse' and the inevitable 'Yes, Mrs Pig'. This game, which I acquired from a colleague, can be adapted to cover a whole range of concepts and themes:

letters, flowers, parts of the body, birds, shapes, colours, furniture, transport and so on. It is an ideal way to capture their attention and gain their active involvement as a group.

Two older children come to collect our register and the day has begun. The children at 4 years old are not yet subject to the jurisdiction of the National Curriculum. At this age they have a limited concentration span and I therefore need to introduce the classroom activities as concisely as possible. They are familiar with some activities and need little or no introduction to them. They know, for example, that only two people at a time from our class (we share some activities and classroom areas with a Year 1 class) can use the sand or play in the pattern house or the Chinese kitchen. Other activities will have been explained previously, or I will expect the children to learn from each other (for example, through computer programs).

We look at a collection of blue objects from around the classroom, at the blues in our clothes and talk about the various shades of blue that we can see. Although they have mixed their own colours before, we recall the processes involved and the things they need to remember. We discuss together what we might learn from the activity and I demonstrate the kinds of patterns they might make with the blues they mix.

I remind them that I hope they will attempt to try all the activities available in the classroom and that we will be talking later about what they have done and found out. Some children will need encouragement to attempt some things and I am aware of those who will avoid some experiences at all costs for whatever reasons. They will need my support to attempt something that they would rather avoid. Given a completely free choice, some children would choose to play in the sand or with the lego all day. I also know that at the end of the day there will be children I have hardly spoken to or been involved with. This is one of the major frustrations of teaching but essential to accept. A teacher can only attempt to make the contacts she does have with each child or group as meaningful and valuable as possible.

I also try to spend some time each day observing the children and the class as a whole. This is probably one of the more difficult things to do as a sense of guilt initially overcomes most teachers when they stop actively teaching and start observing. However, it is of paramount importance if you are to witness the processes of learning taking place. Learning is untidy, hard work, and unpredictable for both children and teachers. Insight gained as a result of reflecting on why a particular incident might have happened can inform future planning and learning. Life in a classroom seldom runs smoothly, no matter how well organised things are: children have disagreements and experience frustrations; things get lost or damaged. All these have learning potential and are part of the rich experience a group of people spending hours together will share. There will be times of elation, success and pleasure, mixed with times of sadness and despair. Young children are amazingly resilient and enthusiastic, taking life at school in their stride, showing a tremendous desire to explore and determination to succeed. It is this drive and enthusiasm which makes them so rewarding to teach.

As children select their initial activities, I move to work with the group of children who have chosen the colour-mixing activity. I watch them to see how they start painting. I talk with them, trying to extend their understanding and develop their skills. Some children will need talking through the whole process, others will work confidently and purposefully. Sometimes I work alongside the children, exploring and demonstrating an activity at my own level. This 'modelling' for the children gives me the opportunity to verbalise my thought processes for them, describing any difficulties or discoveries which I encounter. My 4-year-old shadow is watching everything, occasionally making a comment and asking a question, but determined not to have a go herself. I think that she will when she feels ready.

Next, I join the children who are browsing through books. 'Will you read this to me?' asks one child and I agree. Several other children come to share the story and await their turn to choose. This is an intimate and satisfying time for me and one which the children also seem to enjoy enormously. To have an adult permanently available to share stories and books with the children is ideal and many parents do help them here. As an alternative, we have a whole range of the children's favourite stories on audio tape and they can listen to them using headphones as they turn the pages of the books. Taped stories are a permanent feature of the book corner and the children are taught to operate the tape recorder for themselves.

I pause for a while, as I do frequently, to survey the classroom as a whole. Noticing a child who appears to be upsetting another child who is trying to play a maths game by herself, I go to join them at their table. From watching, it seems that she also wants to play but is being rejected by the solitary child. By starting to play an alternative game I can distract her and engage her interest in something different and so defuse the situation. Alternatively I could have attempted to talk with and share the solitary child's game and, maybe, have involved the other child and encouraged them to play together. There is no *right* way in teaching, but a close relationship with each child, and an increasing understanding of their needs and abilities, can inform the professional judgements and decisions which a teacher makes. My shadow is showing considerable interest in the dice game that I am playing so I ask her to take my turn and find the appropriate card, which she willingly does. Almost without realising, she is actively involved in the game and I am taking the observational role.

I glance at my watch and realise that it is almost time for assembly in the hall. I mention this to the class. Everybody will need to remember what they are doing, leave everything tidily and think about waiting by our classroom door. Some are better at this than others. A few need a gentle reminder or assurance that they will be able to return to their current activity later on. Times like this should not be rushed – all it takes is awareness that a gradual movement towards the door is preferable to a mad rush to be first. Soon we are all assembled and walk quietly to our place in the hall. The headteacher is there and some gentle guitar music is playing as we enter, encouraging us to listen and wait quietly for other classes to arrive.

We start our assembly with a song about the pattern of days in the week, which the children know. We then listen as the headteacher tells us a story which includes the repeating pattern of day and night. The children are asked to think about how this changes from summer to winter and we listen to their ideas and contributions. Birthdays are next and two children, who are 6 and 8 years old respectively, come to the front of the assembly to share this event with us all. We sing our birthday round to them and hear about their presents and feelings. A final hymn is sung and assembly is over. As quietly as we arrived, we return to the classroom and put on our coats, hats and gloves and go outside for playtime. I encourage them to attempt to dress themselves or to help each other. Children who will happily let their parents do this for them are quite capable of managing alone, given time and patience, and it is an important part of their growing independence.

A quick cup of tea and brief exchanges with other teachers in the staff room and two children arrive with a message from the teacher who is on playground duty to tell us that playtime is over. I go to meet my class in the playground as they begin to gather near the classroom door. With their coats and accessories safely returned to their pegs, it is time for the children to have their drinks. Free school milk is a thing of the past, but most children bring a flask with a drink to have at this time of the day. As they finish, they return to the carpeted area to browse through a book or join in with some songs and rhymes with me. When everyone has arrived, we move to the resources room which houses our television and video playback machine to watch and listen to a story called *The Very Hungry Caterpillar* by Eric Carle. I have selected this as it is an animated version of a book which we have recently read in the classroom, and which includes the pattern of days in the week and the cycle of egg to butterfly. The programme also reinforces the letter 'm', which we have learnt how to write and recognise recently. I attempt to link many of the children's learning experiences in a way which will hopefully be meaningful for them. Children extend their understanding and thinking through encountering knowledge, skills and concepts in a variety of different contexts. They also need opportunities to practise and apply skills they have acquired.

Returning to the classroom, the children decide what they will do next. Some return to uncompleted activities while others select something that they have not yet done. I return to the book table to share some more stories, poems and factual books with children. As I circulate around the classroom, I spend five minutes here and there making brief notes of things which the children have said or done, which demonstrate the processes of thinking and learning I have observed. Just before midday, we start to clear the tables ready for lunch. Everybody is expected to help, completing jigsaws, or putting away construction toys and returning books to the bookcases and boxes. When the tables are clear, we meet together on the carpeted area to discuss and share the morning's activities. What have they learned? What did they enjoy or find difficult? Has anyone discovered anything unexpected? We listen to and look at a book a child has made during the morning. Based on the story *The Very Hungry Caterpillar*, the child has worked on it on his own, carefully illustrating the story and attempting the writing by himself. Other children are writing their own simple books and this opportunity to share and review will encourage them to continue and tell them a little more about what makes a book and a story. We notice the title and attractive picture on the front cover alongside his name. This is his story and he is both author and illustrator.

Our dinner lady arrives and it is time for the children to wash their hands, ready for lunch. To avoid a rush to the hand basins, I stagger their departure from the carpeted area. For example, I will ask all the children who are wearing a particular colour or whose name starts with a specific letter to go first. Sometimes, as we wait, I will ask the other children to 'draw' a number or letter in the air or identify one that I draw with my finger on their back. Such five-minute games are an ideal way to reinforce some recent learning or increase their observational skills, as well as being fun to play. As these children are new to the school, they have their lunch in the classroom rather than joining other classes in the dining room. The majority bring a packed lunch in a variety of multi-coloured boxes – Thomas the Tank Engine to Winnie the Pooh! When they return to the classroom, they collect these boxes and settle down to eat. This is a time when I can hand over responsibility to the dinner lady and spend some time reflecting on the morning's teaching and learning. If I do not make notes of significant things which I have heard the children say, or seen them do, then important information showing a child's understanding, emotional state or approach to activities can be lost.

As they finish their meal, the children filter from the classroom into the playground for the remainder of the lunch period. I sometimes choose to share books with individual children at this time as the classroom is quiet and each child can have my undivided attention.

When everybody is outside, my student and I can prepare the tables for the afternoon session. Some learning activities will be the same as during the morning, but one table will be where I start with a group of six children. Easter is approaching and we will spend some time looking at hen's eggs and making meringue nests. The adjacent classroom has an incubator with hen's eggs which are due to hatch in the next couple of days. Our class will be able to share and observe this exciting event.

The room is ready and we leave to have lunch in the staffroom with our colleagues. It is essential to have a break from the classroom and children to unwind and relax in the company of friends. Conversations are wide ranging; sometimes concerned with educational matters but often purely social. I often catch up with events and information with the headteacher at this time.

At 1.25 in the afternoon, we return to our classes. The children are already settling on to the carpeted area, having chosen a book to read. This

is a time when we will all 'read' quietly to ourselves. Even though most of
the children are unable to read to themselves yet, they are capable of
looking at the pictures and using them to help understand the story. My
student and I select a book to read as well so that the children can see us
reading. At this age, a quiet reading period will only last for about five
minutes, but it can gradually be extended as children's reading competence develops. Through this, children begin to perceive reading as
pleasurable and habitual and something which adults engage in regularly.
They also seem to find it a calming experience after the hustle and bustle
of playtime.

We return our books to their appropriate places and think about the
afternoon's activities. I'm always steering them towards work as if it's an
exciting game. I encourage them to think about the morning session and
what particular activities they have still to do. I explain that I will be
starting at the egg table and we move to our respective activities.

I give each child at the table an egg to hold and examine. Next, with a
large sheet of paper and a thick felt-tipped pen, I begin to write down some
of the things they notice about the eggs. 'Mine feels cold and hard', 'It's
bumpy and rolls', 'No, it's not round like a ball'. As they watch me write
down their ideas and comments, they can see where I start to write, how I
form the letters, where one word ends and another begins, that I sometimes
change my mind or make a mistake as I write. As with reading, they can
begin to understand our reasons for writing and see the connection between spoken and written language. Writing becomes not just something
that you do at school, but an essential skill to record our ideas so that we
can share them with others later.

We discuss what might be inside the egg, what is very unlikely to be
inside ('a potato!', 'an elephant!') and then crack one open to see. There is
great potential to develop spoken language through such simple first-hand
experiences. Each child in turn is encouraged to crack open their egg. Of
course, bits of the egg shell get in with the egg and yolks are broken, but all
are learning experiences for these children. We separate the unbroken
yolks from the whites and put all the egg whites into a bowl.

Using a balloon whisk, the children can see bubbles appearing in the
clear albumen; as they beat, more and more small bubbles appear, and the
texture of the egg white changes. They pass the bowl around the table, each
child taking a turn. We add a little sugar: 'What will that do to the egg?'
Other children have arrived to watch and ask questions. More language is
exchanged and explanations given. At this point, I can leave this group
having explained the potential danger of eating raw egg. I will return
periodically to monitor their progress. I move around the classroom joining

children at the sand tray and asking them about the story they are making up about some dinosaurs.

It seems, in no time at all, it is time to clear the tables ready for the afternoon's playtime. Once again, this is a shared responsibility and everybody is expected to help. There are always some children who are reluctant to stop and, if they are very involved with something, I will let them continue until the end of playtime. This playtime is optional and many children prefer to stay inside, sharing books, completing an activity or tidying the room. Chairs are stacked so that tables and floors can be cleaned.

The egg whites and sugar are now stiff and glossy, ready to be transferred as meringues to non-stick vegetable parchment for cooking in the school oven. Cooking is a superb experience for children of this age involving all three core areas of the National Curriculum – science, maths and language – as well as being enjoyable and practical. If parent helpers can be involved in cooking in school, they can see for themselves the value it holds as a learning experience for children.

With playtime over, and the classroom tidy, we gather on the carpet as a class for the last time to review the day's activities and listen to a story. I cannot possibly be aware of everything that has occurred in the classroom during the course of the day, but, given an appropriate time, children can share their experiences and learning. I have made observations and notes during the day about individual children which will become part of ongoing profiles of their progress and stages of development.

The story over, it is time for the children to depart. Parents and friends wait outside the classroom door. Each child is expected to put on their outdoor clothes and collect their belongings. Invariably, there are those who make about three return visits to the classroom to collect their reading folder, drink flask, lunch box or gloves. These are also the apparent dreamers who take forever to get themselves organised and seem unbelievably reluctant to leave.

Finally, everyone has gone and my student and I can spend some time together discussing the day's events and exchanging experiences. For both of us the day will have been totally different, as it will for each child. He has spent time watching and supporting children at the computer, reading books, playing maths games and helping them to make their own books. We can learn and gain insight from each other and in the light of this begin to plan activities for the following day.

There are paintings and pictures to mount and display. A carefully considered display of their work not only helps to create a stimulating environment, but shows the children that we value what they produce. Carefully lettered captions to accompany work provides a potential source for read-ing and a resource bank of words to support their writing. Models and mobiles can hang from strings overhead, making an environment towards which they have created and contributed.

This time spent after school is precious and not always available because of other out-of-school activities. Some teachers run clubs at this time for the older children, there are in-service courses to attend at the local Teacher's Centre and regular in-school meetings. I finally leave the school premises at about 5.30 p.m., but my day is incomplete.

During the evening, I spend some time updating my notes on individual children and their reading record. Otherwise, keeping track of children with whom I have had little contact this particular day is difficult. There are always a few children who demand little attention and could easily slip through the net. If you are aware of who they are, and make a deliberate attempt to engage them more the following day, then you can guard against this.

No day ever runs smoothly. Children fall and hurt themselves or soak themselves in puddles at playtime. They often arrive at school upset for some reason. There are also countless minor classroom interruptions, so my planning for the following day must allow for almost any event. I have my own catastrophe theory. A good teacher plans for catastrophe and hopes some of the plans that take account of yesterday, today and tomor-row will fit the overall term's grand plan. The remainder of the evening is an important time to unwind so my planning for tomorrow must leave me time to relax. Is teaching an exhausting job? Of course it is, but I find that children and their learning are so fascinating that I would not want to be anywhere else.

The hard part is said to be keeping your own integrity intact. I teach because I think the children are worth the effort and that way, the job rewards me rather than wears me out. Tomorrow is never just another day.

Further reading

The story book I referred to in the text is:

Carle, E. (1970) *The Very Hungry Caterpillar*, Puffin Books, London.

5

THE ORGANISATION AND MANAGEMENT OF FIRST SCHOOLS

Peter Gibley

Headteacher, Nelson First School, Norwich

Introduction

Only a few years ago, in the mid-eighties schools were relatively simple places to manage. Headteachers concerned themselves with the children and the curriculum and were responsible for spending only a few thousand pounds of the overall costs of their institutions. Indeed, many of them had no idea what the real costs were of running their schools, for the vast majority of the decisions were taken by officers of the Local Education Authority who did not expect to be consulted about those matters.

This chapter, about school management, must be read with 'change' in mind: vast changes which are affecting every aspect of school life and the headteacher's role within it. The first half of this chapter (up to 'Partnership') is primarily concerned with the recent changes in England and Wales. Scottish and Northern Irish readers should refer to Table 5.1. We will examine many of those changes beginning with the effects of the Education Reform Act 1988 on school management. 'Partnerships' describes the wide range of people commonly found at work in infant schools. 'The Teacher in the Classroom' discusses some methods of organising an infant class and its associated workload. 'Some Additional Responsibilities' describes some related tasks in and around the classroom. The Conclusion emphasises the personal contribution a teacher makes towards children's development.

At the time of writing, we are in the midst of a host of changes and their effects are, as yet, by no means clear. While it is not the purpose of this chapter to do more than describe the processes of school and class management, it is necessary to say that there are still many difficulties which remain unresolved for schools.

Perhaps, in a few years time, when the revolution is completed, many

	Scotland	Northern Ireland
Who has financial responsibility for ongoing running costs of a school?	The Regional Council	The Education and Library Board
Who ensures that the curriculum is provided in a school?	Regional Council, School Board and the Chairman of the School Board	School Board of Governors and the Principal
Who sits on the above boards?	Parents, teachers and co-opted members to represent the community	*Controlled schools*: 4 nominated by Transferors, 2 elected by parents, 2 chosen by Education and Library Board, 1 elected by the teachers. *Maintained schools*: 6 nominated by Trustees, 2 elected by the Education and Library Board, 1 elected by the parents and 1 elected by the teachers
Who employs the school staff?	The Regional Council	*Controlled schools*: the Education Board. *Maintained schools*: Council for Catholic Maintained Schools
Who chooses which school a child should attend?	The child's parents	The child's parents
What limits the size of a school's intake?	Physical capacity of the school	Physical capacity of the school
Addresses for further information	The Scottish Education Department New St Andrew's House, Edinburgh EH1 3SY	Department of Education for Northern Ireland, Rathgael House, Balloo Road, Bangor, BT19 2PR

Table 5.1 Brief summary of school management in Scotland and Northern Ireland

of the problems we are facing now will have dissipated: presently, many feel that there are just too many reforms tumbling upon schools at too fast a rate and with too few resources being made available for training, to ensure the effective introduction of them all.

Headteachers in the primary field cannot be removed from any aspect of school life. At precisely the moment when the burden of training and implementation of the newly born National Curriculum has fallen up them, the Education Reform Act (1988) has changed school management fundamentally.

The Education Act (1988)

We have seen how, prior to this Act, decisions over most of a school's range of activities were made by the Local Education Authority (LEA). At a stroke the government shifted the power: but that power was not simply vested in the schools. To find where it has been placed it is necessary to understand that each school in the maintained (i.e. State) sector has, as its constitutional basis, Articles of Government. These appear in schools as rule books which set out the legal basis of the establishment and the governing body's composition and responsibilities. The Government's rewritten Articles have given the funding and the power to the governors of individual schools. A good example is found in the employment terms of teachers: nowadays they are appointed by the governors, with the local authority playing, at most, an advisory role.

At the same time, the composition of the governing body has been redefined, removing the political emphasis and placing parents, teachers, and those with a direct interest in the school, in controlling positions.

Originally it was intended that only secondary and very large primary schools should be devolved, that is, manage their own budgets. Establishments with devolved status have a wide range of control of their own affairs in a landlord–tenant relationship with their local authorities. However, the field has been extended so that, now, nearly every school within the maintained sector can choose to have its own budget.

It was no easy job for LEAs to decide just how much money should go to each shool. The 1988 Act established that a formula should be devised and that the majority of the money should be generated according to the number of pupils in each school. Local authorities have approached this with varying degrees of enthusiasm! The first authorities, some three years ago, devised a simple system and split the money up among as many of their schools as they possibly could. Other authorities took their time in order to devise a forumla which reflected the individual needs of schools, with their varying localitites and problems, and they are now applying their new formulae in steadily phased manners. Thus, in 1991, it is quite usual to find many schools in differing situations within an LEA. All may, indeed, have a formula-generated budget yet some remain under LEA control, while others are completely devolved, running their affairs under the landlord–tenant relationship already described. However, this is far from all the picture!

Schools have now been invited, through the mechanism of a prescribed programme of governor and parent ballots, to decide whether they wish to opt out completely from local authority involvement and be funded directly from central government. The school can then receive all the money which its formula generates, plus the share that would have been retained by the LEA for their erstwhile provision of central services. Schools which opt out in this way are known as 'grant-maintained' and they would seem to represent a further logical development of the shifting of power. Clearly though, opting out presents a big decision, for a grant-maintained school has to stand on its own feet: it must make financial provision for all the services it needs, many of which the LEA has traditionally provided. For example, it will have to pay for the support of the psychologist or the educational welfare officer and the preparation of its monthly payroll. Presently, there are very few schools in England and Wales which have grant-maintained status but there are very many more which are examining the option seriously and which may become grant-maintained in the next few months and years.

We have seen how, in all these situations, the power has shifted very significantly. Consider where this leaves the headteacher and the staff. Although headteachers have the option to be governors of their own schools, we observe that all this new power has not been placed in their hands: indeed they have become paid servants of their schools, appointed by the governors themselves.

While, in practice, few governing bodies would wish to function without the fullest support and co-operation of their headteachers, the ultimate power and responsibility now lies with this lay body, elected largely by the school's parents.

Schools necessarily work in a combination of different timespans. Educational years run from September to August, while financial years in schools follow the business year and extend from April to March. At some time in the early months of the new calendar year, heads begin to assemble budgetary information. They need to know, as soon as possible, how much money they will have for the new financial year which will start in April. They also need to monitor their current spending so that they can identify money to finance the really important decisions about staffing and the admission policy for the next academic year. If they have spent too much money this year it won't be apparent for some time, so there is an element of forecasting, and even guesswork in the school's planning for the following September. Budgetary success depends, more than ever, on comprehensive and accurate information being promptly made available and many schools have introduced sophisticated information technology into their offices to help them cope.

Many of these new difficulties and challenges arise largely from the speed with which the changes have been brought about and the widely varying amounts of training made available for heads and administrative staff. Schools with few office resources and limited secretarial hours have been hit harder by this revolution: other schools, particularly the larger ones, have always needed efficient and separate administrative units and have generally coped rather better.

Cost is a crucial factor in every consideration. A new teaching appointment is now made on a completely different basis. You will frequently hear teachers refer to themselves as 'expensive' or worse still 'cheap'! For not only do teachers come in all physical shapes and sizes, but they vary widely in their employment contracts and obligations. Whatever is 0.3 of a teacher? Head and shoulders, perhaps, or the best part of both legs! In fact, schools employ as many teachers as they can possibly afford and a fraction of a teacher is calculated in terms of contact hours with the children. Thus, 0.1 is roughly half a day's work, 0.2 is a whole day, and so on. It's up to schools how they best use those hours: one part-timer may be in school every day for a few hours, while another, working the same number of hours, may not appear at all on two days of the week but be there for the majority of the other three days.

All teachers are paid on the same salary scale but they may be at widely different points on it and so be receiving different amounts of money at the end of each month. Deputy Heads and headteachers have separate pay scales and, under the new pay regulations, they are free to negotiate their own salaries, within certain limits.

It is, therefore, of paramount budgetary importance that schools nowadays know the exact cost of each member of staff for, in order to stay within their new budgets, they may have to release an expensive teacher and appoint a much more economical probationer (i.e. a teacher in their first year of work) or another younger colleague to do the same job. The introduction of individual school budgets has meant that more teachers have had to move to other schools and more voluntary and compulsory redundancies have occurred.

It is unfortunate that such radical financial reforms have been introduced at a time of such relatively tight funding throughout the education service, for the effectiveness of the reforms themselves has been seriously hampered by a general lack of cash earmarked specifically for their implementation. Special budgetary arrangements have had to be made for smaller schools, many of them rural, to ensure their survival and to meet their legitimate needs.

As more and more schools move away from the LEA it becomes more difficult to provide central services. Many of these services have evolved over the years to meet the needs of the community, for example libraries and youth orchestras and their futures are in the balance. Further, there are services which the local authority has to provide by statute: the assessment and resourcing of children with special educational needs and the maintenance of a local inspectorate are current examples. The Department of Education is pressing LEAs to reduce still further the proportion of money held centrally and to share it out to schools. It seems that the future LEA will respond in two parallel ways. First it will have to maintain its statutory role, whatever that turns out to be. Secondly, it may provide a range of services, in open competition with commercial organisations, and charge realistic prices for them.

It has not been possible to describe the nature of school management without comtemplating, in some detail, the morass of current changes and developments. Everything, from window cleaning to grasscutting and staff training, has become the educational manager's legitimate business and, more importantly, it all has a pricetag newly attached!

It is clear that the governing body has become similar to the board of a company, with the headteacher usually occupying a seat on that board as managing director. Medium-sized schools are now medium-sized companies with annual budgets in excess of half-a-million pounds and with thirty or forty staff on their payrolls. While many of the managerial skills required are no different to those in other kinds of organisations, it is worth observing that many of the headteachers who will carry these new educational companies into the twenty-first century were appointed to do very different jobs.

Advertising and marketing

The main impetus behind the radical reform of school management has been the government's strong belief that competition raises standards. We have already observed that schools receive most of their money according to the number of pupils on their rolls. In order to make competition possible it was necessary to introduce 'open enrolment', thereby removing catchment areas as we knew them. In effect, parents became free to send their children to any school with the space to accept them, provided they make any necessary transport arrangements for themselves.

A school may only refuse to admit a child if it can show that it has insufficient space. The maximum number of children permitted in each school is set by the LEA and remains one of its statutory responsibilities. Many schools are currently operating with numbers well below their permitted maximums. More pupils mean more money and, in industrial terms, one way to increase turnover is to increase input, which, for schools, means finding more children. Schools cannot create more children, so an increase in one school must mean a reduction in another.

In times past, most children were placed in their neighbourhood schools but the new spirit of competition now encourages schools to market themselves efficiently in order to present an attractive image to their many extra potential customers. School brochures are, therefore, becoming glossy prospectuses, advertising appears in corridors and concert programmes and attractive advertisements are being taken in the local press.

When enterprising schools have approached the business world they have often received warm welcomes. Potential markets have been readily identified for many products. Sponsorship deals have already included the provision of all kinds of equipment, ranging from minibuses to sports kit and eager sponsors have paid for diverse projects and publications. Commercial logos have appeared on school letterheads and hoardings have been placed in some school grounds. Financial inducements, in the form of discounted goods, have been offered to those parents who enrol their children at a particular school!

Some determined companies are training their staff to become school governors in order to promote their firm's interests and perhaps to ensure a steady recruitment of school-leavers.

The spirit of open competition coupled with the legal requirement to publish examination results have prompted some headteachers to place advertisements in the press, making bold claims about their school's prowess.

All this activity is having a considerable effect upon the perceptions of parents and children, and we must pause to consider how they, the clients, are to make the best choices? Has selecting a school been made any easier? Indeed, how are students in the teaching profession itself to decide which school best suits them? Many professional associations and LEAs are currently drawing up voluntary codes of conduct which seek to set sensible constraints upon the activities of schools within the difficult areas of mar-

keting and advertising. While no one wishes to see good practices elimi-
nated, many are recognising that not all the activities of commerce are
appropriate for the world of education.

Thus, guiding principles are emerging. For example, present pupils
should not be disadvantaged by their school's commercial activities, and no
claim should be made on behalf of one school which denigrates the work of
another. While it is possible for a school to claim that its examination
results are outstanding it should be done without boasting that it is 'the best
in the neighbourhood'. For, as long as schools very properly must admit
children of varying abilities without exercising any selection, direct comparisons will remain extremely difficult to make.

In the absence of an independent council, which would set standards for
the whole profession and regulate the behaviour of those within it, only a
court of law can presently decide whether the marketing behaviour of a
particular school is right and proper. We await the first case with interest
for, as governors make these decisions and respond to the pressures of
declining rolls or imminent staffing cuts, there will surely be one. We can
hardly expect our governors to leave their newly found freedoms in the
filing cabinet!

Full devolution, grant-maintained status and open enrolment are in their
infancy and at the moment the media-men have only a toe in the door. But
observe the bulging marketing portfolios under their arms and the eager
smiles upon their faces!

Partnerships

No matter how the funding arrives, schools remain unshakeably about
people. One simply can't avoid them! Children are everywhere, of course,
but threaded through and around them, are many different kinds of people.
Let's look at some of them more closely.

Teachers

Teachers are, obviously, the key figures but their management role is so
much greater that it will be considered in more depth later in this chapter.

Parents

Parents, too, are central figures educationally: they may be governors (see
above), paid or unpaid helpers (see below), or closely involved partners

who, though they spend little time in school, nevertheless keep in close contact with their children's learning activities.

Support staff

Most schools have a degree of paid welfare support within their classrooms. It may not be much: in many infant departments just one person is spread thinly over all the classes, while in some rarer instances, each teacher has a full-time welfare assistant! It may be that this person is principally a well-meaning, sympathetic character who is particularly adept at cuts and bruises, but many welfare asistants are qualified nursery nurses and are capable of close involvement in all aspects of the teacher's work. This is very often true of those who are supporting children with special needs, whose difficulties may be physical, mental or emotional and who gain considerably from the services of their experienced and knowledgeable welfare assistants.

Elsewhere in school, the office may be occupied by a secretary on a full-time basis, or in smaller establishments, the welfare assistant may double as secretary, for a very few hours each week.

Other paid staff

Around the school, at various times, may be midday supervisory assistants (MSAs), cooks and kitchen staff who, between them, deal with the whole business of serving and clearing up lunch as well as keeping order in the playground and classrooms throughout the whole midday break.

The school will be cleaned before or after sessions and sometimes during teaching time, too. As well as cleaning staff, there may be a full-time caretaker who can perform a wide range of additional functions, including security and maintenance work.

If the school is lucky enough to have a swimming pool, there may be a paid instructor. Nearby, there may be a salaried road crossing patrol helping the children to get to and from school safely.

Unpaid helpers

Many schools have far more voluntary helpers than paid staff. Real partnerships commonly flourish between schools and parents, many of whom make regular and clear commitments to support their children's learning, at school and at home. It may be that they help with reading and language work but their efforts may be directed towards any activity. Some schools start the day with quiet reading times when all parents are encouraged to stay and share books with their youngsters. Parents cook, sew, make models and help with swimming and games. They also paint and assist on outings and visits: in fact, they can be found everywhere! At best, these partnerships are relaxed and comfortable, being universally recognised as of enormous benefit to the children.

Governors, too, are increasingly evident during the schoolday as they acquaint themselves more closely with the busy workplaces they are now charged with managing.

The school may cast its net widely over the whole community, luring those with talents and businesses to volunteer their services to enrich the children's learning. A potter may work regularly with groups of children and local professional sportsmen of many kinds inspire young players on school fields.

Teachers themselves may visit neighbouring schools, to share ideas and to link up with nurseries and playgroups, or with the schools to which the children will transfer when they are older. The local policeman may be a frequent visitor, perhaps taking part in a planned programme of work about safety.

At the heart of this busy human kaleidoscope is the class teacher! So many individuals moving around, across, and even over one another, may often cause the classroom to resemble a beehive. The teacher's thorough planning and sense of overall direction, however, ensure that the workers in the classroom are as purposeful as those in the hive!

The teacher in the classroom

In discussing the nature and purpose of the class teacher's job we might find no difficulty in agreeing that a major aspect of the role must be to maximise learning opportunities for each individual child. Teachers of young children can't fail to recognise that each child makes different responses at different speeds and has widely varying needs.

It follows that, for much of the time, a good infant classroom may have a variety of activities going on simultaneously. For, even when all the children start the same activity together, they will each finish it at very different times: the first child may complete a picture in thirty seconds, while the last little worker adds minute details tirelessly and beavers away all morning! Those who have finished first will need other things to do and it's only a matter of time before their teacher decides that it is more productive to run several well-planned activities side by side and to spread the children around them.

This kind of integration, perhaps with regular groupings, is common in many primary schools, but the real 'integrated day' is a rarity. In this case, each child moves through a web of linked activities and the teacher monitors progress and adapts and modifies activities accordingly. No two children necessarily follow the same route, but the teacher ensures that each achieves a balanced educational diet in the end. Even in this method the class will still be drawn together frequently, perhaps just to top and tail sessions or to share a common theme or starting point. It's rare, however, to find an effective infant class where the children sit for very large chunks of time listening to their teacher: active learning is very much the order of the day!

Teachers plan extensively from many sources. They consult the new National Curriculum syllabuses, arrange for live or recorded TV and radio programmes, delve into banks of visual and literary resources, both in and out of school, and refer constantly to the school's own guidelines and schemes of work.

They may consult with colleagues informally or plan closely together as team teachers having shared classes in one larger teaching space. These teachers may take the opportunity to bring children together from each class and to take larger groups for more genreal activities such as games or drama. Stories and music may be shared, too: indeed, the educational work may be so dovetailed between the classes that the children come to regard both teachers as important to them and move easily between them.

After the children have gone home, teachers have a variety of things to do. First, there's a range of children's work to tackle: pictures, models, science and discovery work, stories and poems perhaps and all in various stages of completion! Some must be mounted and displayed, others may already be in books, but each piece will receive some kind of attention. This process helps to establish the starting points for tomorrow, as judgements are formed about children's progress.

Written records of individuals will be updated and notes made of significant events that occurred during the day. Appointments will be kept with the headteacher and other colleagues to discuss learning difficulties and possible referrals to outside agencies for extra help. After school may also be the time to arrange the visit to the museum or to track down the elusive microscope for tomorrow.

Parents may be interviewed privately to discuss the general progress of their child or to share a particular problem which may best be tackled together. Contact with parents has other purposes, too, and may be organised across the whole school or in year groups. Parents need to know, and have a right to understand, what schools are doing with their children and most schools take this very seriously. Open days and evenings are organised, and workshops or more formal talks and discussions take place from time to time. Not only do schools wish to show the activities in the school at their best but headteachers are also keen to interpret and explain modern developments and legislation which may affect children greatly. For example, although no single subject arouses parent passions more quickly than reading, many schools have undergone major revolutions in its methodology without difficulty by carrying the parents with them, perhaps through a series of active adult workshops.

A good infant school sees itself as an early link in a lengthy educational chain and understandings gained by parents may inform vital decisions later. Of course, it does not escape headteachers that truly open schools, seeking to serve their parents well, offer attractive images to potential consumers!

Unfortunately, formal staff meetings are traditionally held in this precious time after school, too! They are supported by training days, usually about five in number, spread throughout the year. The staff may be in school without the children on these additional days, or several schools may cluster together and follow a specified and agreed training programme.

It is through meetings of all kinds that whole school approaches are identified and developed. The headteacher, who may have a considerable teaching commitment, is likely to be the one person who can maintain an overview and can encourage the staff to establish the school's general aims and ideals together, and to put them into practice. Indeed, the social climate needs careful tending, for although delicately constructed, it is of crucial importance: making possible, as it should, vital co-operation and mutual support. At its best, a supportive emotional climate encourages risk-taking and innovation; essential features in successful active learning.

Staff may decide to plan projects across the whole school or year groups, and the headteacher will be concerned to see that the right resources are available and used efficiently. The first colleague to reach the school library may need dissuading from swiping all the best source books for just their one class!

New teachers need a special kind of care and each school has a responsibility to provide it. I would expect some regular, planned release from the classroom to be offered to the probationer, in order that there is time for proper reflection and support.

A successful staff needs to take part in a whole range of outside courses as well as running its own profesisonal training in school. So the staffroom may be a very busy place: some colleagues being away on short or long courses while others are collaborating on a piece of research within the school: something always seeming to be going on!

Continuity, in content and standards of work, has become a major priority and, at primary level, it is probably the headtacher who leads the staff in devising systems which record and help to assess children's progress. The new colleague should fit into the staffroom chemistry happily, gaining support and encouragement and contributing enthusiasm and new thinking.

The National Curriculum has brought with it formal testing at the ages of 7, 11 and 14. The assessment is, at the moment, two-pronged: teacher assessment, prepared within the school from detailed records and evidence, and an externally set series of tasks in English, maths and science: the subjects which together comprise 'the core curriculum'. Six- and seven-year olds have been tested for the first time in the Summer term, 1991.

Lastly, teachers' contracts of employment now include their participation in a new scheme of appraisal. The government is committed to the introduction of a full system and teachers are understandably nervous about it. At best, it must proceed in a spirit of trust and mutual support: one can only urge that sufficient time and resources are made available so that this delicate matter can be put in place smoothly.

Some additional responsibilities for the teacher

Having dealt at some length with the educational aspects of a teacher's work, I must mention one important and overriding responsibility. The primary teacher's paramount concern must be for the safety and welfare of the children. Around the classroom, scissors and wet areas present obvious safety problems but other dangers abound: damaged furniture, or an open cupboard door, may be the cause of an avoidable accident.

This concern extends out of school to road safety and to all aspects of survival in the busy world. Every school should now have a health and safety representative: it's probably the headteacher!

It's possible, too, that the teacher may be just the person to help a child to cope with racial and social difficulties, where they arise naturally.

The management of other people's money is a daily problem for the teacher: it's inevitable that large amounts of it cross the desk! There's dinner money and outing money and payments for uniform and sales of all kinds. The school may hold charity events and will, almost certainly, raise funds for itself. School photographers are frequent visitors and generate very large sums of money.

A further managerial task occurs each day. The attendance register has to be completed accurately, and numbers taken for lunch. On most mornings the teacher receives important notes and messages from home and, at the end of the day, has to ensure that the right books, kit, lunch boxes, clothes and letters go home with each child! Sadly, lost property presents a perpetual challenge. The child may not recognise her own vest, the teacher can only guess at the right one, but the mother will unerringly retrieve her own child's garment from ten seemingly identical items!

Most schools, however, have good management systems for these tricky administrative areas, and teachers do develop their own pretty quickly. They realise that a crowded and busy classroom can only be managed well with a high degree of organisation. It's not good enough just to survive: teachers must somehow stay fresh and enthusiastic at their work. It's such a shame when, after a sensitive day in the classroom, a row with a parent over a lost sock sends a teacher home dispirited and leads the parent to value all the work of that teacher rather less.

That so many teachers operate, day after day, with energy and vitality, often reaching inspirational heights, is a reflection of the unquenchable dedication so often encountered throughout the profession.

Conclusion

School and class management systems are not ends in themselves. They exist to promote efficiency: but they should support invisibly, much as do concrete foundations which, though quite substantial, underpin a building without being seen.

It is natural for a student or new teacher to find some of the organisation at school too prominent and daunting. In time, good systems will be absorbed and slip into the background, freeing the teacher to encourage those myriad small miracles to arise in the classroom, achieved by fascinated and active children, working confidently under good school management.

6
REFORMING THE CURRICULUM

Vivienne Gray

Visiting Tutor at University of East Anglia

The Education Reform Act (ERA) of 1988 has brought about the most sweeping changes in schools in England and Wales since the reforms at the end of the Second World War. Similar changes have occurred in Scotland and Northern Ireland, which are briefly documented in Table 6.1

In 1944 an Education Act determined the structure of schooling that most of today's adults have experienced. They have grown up in a system which, although it has been modified, has not altered radically since that date.

Historical background

The 1944 Act stated the aim of providing an education according to the three 'A's – age, ability and aptitude – for all pupils, and as such it reflected the social concerns of a nation looking ahead to a future of peace and hoped-for prosperity. It is worth remembering that the late 1940s also saw the birth of the National Health Service and the growth of new towns such as Stevenage in Hertfordshire. A population enjoying better health care and housing needed an education service to match, and the 1944 Act laid the foundations for this, although certain provisions were altered as time went by. The school leaving age was raised from 14 to 15 in 1947, and to 16 in 1972, as the value of educational opportunities became more widely recognised. In most areas of England and Wales the 11-plus examination, leading to selective secondary schooling, was also abolished and comprehensive schooling gradually introduced.

During the 1970s, however, there was much questioning of the role of the education service. The mood of the country had changed, and education

	Scotland	Northern Ireland
Areas of Study covered in curricular guidelines	English Mathematics Environmental sciences (includes science, technology, history, geography and health) Expressive Arts (music, art, drama and physical education) Religious, Moral and Social Education	English Mathematics Science and Technology (includes design) Environment and Society (history and geography) Creative and Expressive Studies (art and design, music and physical education) Irish (in Irish-speaking schools)

Additional information	The guidelines allow for a flexibility element of 20% of available curricular time for the on-schools' enhancement or reinforcement of particular curricular areas or activities at different ages or stages; for learning support and enrichment: for whole school activities, or for opportunities for learning which may arise from contemporary events or issues.	All schools must provide Religious Education. In addition to the compulsory subjects listed above there are four cross-curricular themes which will also be compulsory
		i.e. Education for Mutual Understanding
		    Cultural Heritage
		    Health Education
		    Information Technology

Details of Assessment	Scottish Standardised Tests are taken by primary 4 (8-year-old) pupils in March and April. The children take a test in English (reading and writing) and a test in mathematics. Each test is made up of four units which can be taken at different times and last about 20 minutes each. The 5–14 Programme in Scotland uses five levels (A–E) to describe attainment targets for pupils as they move through the primary school and into the first two years of secondary school. Teachers in Primary 4 will assess their pupils throughout the year and decide at which level each child should be assessed in the Standardised Tests. Most pupils in P4 should be able to attain level B and some will reach level C. The tests are administered, and marked, by the school. The Scottish Office describes them as 'very like normal classwork.'[1]	Assessment will be introduced for pupils at the end of Key Stage 1 (i.e. 8-year-olds) in 1993/94. Most subjects which are compulsory during that key stage will be assessed with the exception of those within the Creative and Expressive areas of study. The form of assessment is still to be decided (1991).
For further information write to:	The Scottish Education Department New St Andrew's House Edinburgh EH1 3SY	Department of Education for Northern Ireland Rathgael House Balloo Road Bangor County Down BNT19 2PR

Table 6.1 Curriculum and assessment arrangements for the early years of schooling in Scotland and Northern Ireland (1991)
(1) *Primary Testing: A Guide for Parents*

was seen more and more as a servant of the economy. The old post-war ideals had been expensive to implement, and the concept of a system offering unlimited opportunity with no visible return was no longer acceptable. In 1976, the Labour Prime Minister, James Callaghan, made a famous speech at Ruskin College. He criticised teachers for not helping to encourage the scientists and technicians who would be needed for an increasingly complex and mechanised society. Within eleven years of that speech, plans were being drawn up by the (then Conservative) government for a National Curriculum (NC) which would emphasise the acquisition of a 'core' of knowledge and skills. Implementation of this curriculum became statutory with the passing of the Act in 1988.

This then, is a brief description of the historical background to the legislation. Kelly (1990) and Brighouse and Moon (1990), in their useful books on the National Curriculum, give much more detail and are well worth reading.

The ERA encompasses a wide range of radical reforms, including the introduction of Local Management of Schools (LMS) and of compulsory Assessment of children's learning. LMS has been dealt with elsewhere in the publication, so this chapter will concentrate on the subject matter and assessment arrangements laid down in the Act.

National Curriculum subjects

The ERA (see glossary of terms on page 76) lays down a 'curriculum entitlement' for every child in state education in England and Wales. This consists of a 'core curriculum' of english, mathematics and science. In addition there are 'foundation subjects' of technology, history, geography, art, music, PE and modern foreign languages. Religious education (RE), which since 1944 has been the only statutory subject, has been retained alongside the National Curriculum as equivalent to a foundation subject. However, the management of RE is still the responsibility of Local Education Authorities (LEAs), who are required to provide syllabuses and in-service training of teachers (INSET). Each LEA must be supported by a Standing Advisory Council on Religious Education (SACRE).

In Wales, Welsh is also a core subject in schools where Welsh is spoken. In non-Welsh-speaking schools, it is a foundation subject. Originally the distinction between core and foundation subjects was less marked, but as it became apparent that the school timetable could not cope with an equal emphasis on all subjects, there was a shift towards the present arrangement. It could also prove too expensive to resource all subjects to an acceptable level. Many primary schools, for instance, were ill-equipped for the demands of the Science NC.

It is evident from this list that preference has been given to what is often termed 'basic skills' subjects. In part this is a response to the call for a better-trained workforce for the future, as education comes more and more under central government control. It may also be a consequence of the tremendous expansion of educational opportunity since 1944. The raising of the school leaving age resulted in a huge increase in further and higher education, typified by the 'redbrick' universities and Open University as well as poly-technic colleges. A better-educated populace is naturally going to aspire to even better opportunities for the next generation, and to be more critical of the system in place. This is true, too, in other spheres of life. Housing comforts such as indoor sanitation, bathrooms and central heating are com-monplace today but were far from standard in many homes in 1944. Similarly, sophisticated surgery techniques in hospitals have led to a demand for ever more improvements and innovations in surgical medicine.

So perhaps it is important to remember that an education system for all has only been available since the 1870 Education Act. In that 120 years educational opportunities have expanded at a rate undreamed of in the Victorian era. Descendants of those who entered menial employment at a young age are now able to pursue their education to degree level or beyond if they have the inclination and ability. It is more likely to be financial than educational deficiencies that prevent them so doing.

Nevertheless, the call for a better education system has led to the National Curriculum, which is seen by many as the way to raise standards in the nation's schools. The 'basic skills' subjects have been given pride of place and teachers are getting to grips with the new ways of working, which includes learning a bewildering vocabulary of phrases and acronyms, some-times known as 'NCSpeak'! A brief guide to the most commonly used initials and abbreviations can be found at the end of this chapter. Although this vocabulary seems confusing at first, it does give the advantage of a common language which makes communication among professionals more effective. The disadvantage is that after years of opening up schools to parents and involving them in an educational partnership, a 'jargon barrier' is now in place. Teachers will therefore have to ensure that parents are not alienated. *The National Curriculum – A Survival Guide for Parents* by Merttens and Vass (1989) was one of the first attempts to present essential information in a clear, easily accessible format, and is worth looking at.

Organisation of subjects

At the time of writing the only subjects where Statutory Orders are fully in place are English, mathematics, science and technology. History and geographty are due to be implemented in September, 1991, with other foundation subjects to follow in 1992. All subject content has been drawn up in consultation with members of the National Curriculum Council (NCC) who have advised the government throughout. Interim Reports, Consultation Reports, Proposals and Draft Orders have been circulated by the Department of Education and Science (DES) over a period of time, to allow educationists and other interested parties to comment. The final say, however, has been with the Secretary of State for Education in each case.

There have been three Secretaries of State during this period – Kenneth Baker, John MacGregor and Kenneth Clarke – each of whom has left his own mark on the proceedings. Kenneth Baker was the original architect of the ERA, while John MacGregor and Kenneth Clarke had the responsibility of modifying the original plans in the light of early experience. It is likely that more modifications will take place before the entire NC is implemented.

The documents

Each subject has an NC Document, presented in ring binder format so that additions can be made if necessary. Subject matter is divided into Attainment Targets (ATs), varying in number in the original documents from fourteen (mathematics) to three (history). In part this reflects the changes that have occurred as the documents evolved – the History Interim Report, for instance, had five ATs – but it also reflects the priorities of the various NC teams. The first edition Mathematics ATs have titles like '*Measures*' (AT 8) or '*Shape and Space*' (ATs 10 and 11), while the History AT 2 is entitled '*Interpretations of History*'. The Science Document originally had a mammoth seventeen ATs, but these were reduced to nine after much criticism.

In May 1991, following consultation, the DES issued two further documents which set out new Proposals for Mathematics and Science. The original ATs were so numerous in these subjects that they proved 'an obstacle to manageable and sound testing, and intelligible reporting to parents' (DES, May 1991 Proposals, Mathematics and Science). It is now suggested that there be only five ATs in each of these subjects, with consequent grouping of some of the old ATs. These are to be called New Attainment Targets (NATs). The intention is that the Order arising from these Proposals shall come into force from 1 August 1992.

It should be evident from this that many more changes could still occur as the National Curriculum is fully implemented in all subject areas; in fact the ATs can be reviewed at any time. The ATs are what the Act defines as the 'knowledge, skills and understanding' which pupils are expected to have by the end of each Key Stage (ages 7, 11, 14, and 16). It is not expected that all pupils will be at the same stage in their learning, and so each AT will be assessed on a ten-level scale covering the period of compulsory schooling (ages 5–16). This will be discussed in greater detail later in the chapter.

In addition to the ATs, the documents contain Programmes of Study (PoS), defined in the Act as the 'matters, skills and processes' which are required to be taught to pupils to enable them to meet the ATs. There is considerable variation in the way in which PoS are set out in different documents, again reflecting the advice of the different NC teams. Although the PoS are not the first pages in the Document, they provide an overview of each subject and indeed some teachers prefer to move them to the front of the binder for initial reference when planning schemes of work.

The next section of each Document contains the Non-Statutory Guidance (NSG), which is designed to support the teaching of each subject. It discusses such issues as planning, implementation, progression and continuity. In some cases the information in this section has been superceded by later publications from the NCC.

Apart from a copy of the legal details surrounding the NC, there is also a section on National Curriculum Assessment Arrangements for KS1 which have become statutory during the academic year 1990–1991. Originally it was intended that all subjects should be formally assessed at each KS, but following a pilot scheme in the summer of 1990, it was realised that this was, in practice, unworkable. Consequently the assessment plans have been trimmed drastically and only English, mathematics and science will be formally assessed, with results reported to parents. Assessment arrangements have become the responsibility of the School Examinations and Assessment Council (SEAC), which took over from the earlier Task Group on Assessment and Testing (TGAT), and which advises the government on all aspects of assessment.

Assessment at the Key Stages

The results of assessment must be reported back to parents at Key Stages 1–4 (ages 7, 11, 14 and 16). Teachers of pupils in the early years of schooling need concern themselves only with KS1 for the most part. However, it is important to know something of the KS2 requirements as some first schools take children up to the age of 8 or 9 when children would already be working towards KS2.

During the academic year 1990–91, all KS1 children in maintained schools were assessed, firstly by Teacher Assessments (TAs) which took place in the Spring term. School staff were given training by LEAs in observing, gathering evidence and monitoring pupil performance.

Subsequently, pupils were given Standard Assessment Tasks (SATs) devised by a consortium from various educational establishments. The SATs were administered in the first half of the Summer term, and had to be completed by the end of May, 1991. They were concerned only with the core subjects of English, mathematics and science, and led to Statements of Attainment (SoAs) at AT levels 1–3 for the KS1 pupils. The original Statutory Orders for Science contain a total of 409 SoAs, so it is not surprising that the modifications mentioned earlier have been demanded by teachers who found the system unworkable. The new Proposals outline only 178 SoAs for science, while the mathematics SoAs are to be reduced from 296 to 147.

Key Stage 1

Pupils at KS1 are expected to be able in the main to achieve Level 2 SoAs. As mentioned before, there are ten levels of attainment in each subject. Eighty per cent of Year 2 (KS1) children are expected to achieve Level 2 SoAs, with ten per cent achieving Level 1 and ten per cent achieving Level 3. In 1991, teachers of Year 2 children (that is, children who reached the age of 7 years between 1 September 1990 and 31 August 1991) were issued with SAT packs containing instructions, assessment sheets and guidance notes to help them with the SATs. These were intimidating documents for some people, and the assessment procedures caused many problems. Lack of time was one of the main complaints, but there were also difficulties with resources. In some cases the children not being assessed in the class had to 'mark time' with routine tasks in order to free the teacher for the small group work demanded by the SATs.

In view of the trial nature of the 1991 SATs, teachers were given the opportunity to provide feedback to LEA advisers, and this in turn has been passed on to the DES. It is hoped in the future that a more realistic assessment timetable and workload will be implemented.

Profiling and Records of Achievement

The assessment procedure does not stop at recording the results of assessment. The results of TAs and SATs have to be summarised and aggregated, with the SAT results having more importance. The results then go to determine Profile Component (PC) levels. PCs are made up of ATs or groups of ATs which form a 'strand' of a subject, hence in English there are 3 PCs: Speaking and Listening (AT1); Reading (AT2); Writing (ATs 3–5). The purpose of this is to put together a profile or Record of Achievement (RoA). The Record will contain assessments of a pupil's 'work, skills, abilities, personal qualities' (p. 5, *Records of Achievement in Primary Schools*, SEAC, 1990). Samples of work undertaken throughout the year can be included so that an overall picture of the pupil can be built up, which in turn forms the basis of a written report on that pupil. There is a legal requirement for this written report (which must contain the results of any statutory assessments as well as information about other subjects and school activities) to be made to the parents or guardians of each pupil by the end of the school year.

Parents and the National Curriculum

The ERA clearly sets out to involve parents far more in their children's education. Reporting in written form to children in first or infant schools has not been the norm, although parents have had opportunities to discuss their children's progress at open evenings arranged by schools on an *ad hoc* basis. It has no doubt been the case in the past that some teachers have written fairly judgemental comments in their private notes, knowing that the audience for these notes would be limited to themselves and colleagues. So a more formalised and open reporting system should lead to more objective and effective profiles. Until the first batch of these new-style reports has been deliverd, and parents' reactions have been evaluated, we shall not know if the ERA has achieved what it set out to do at least in the context of the National Curriculum.

Its aims in this context are to offer entitlement to a broad and balanced spread of curriculum subjects, to ensure assessment in these subjects at regular intervals, and to make the results of assessment available to parents or guardians. Partnership between home and school has always been important in the most enlightened infant and first schools, but the legislation makes it very difficult for any schools to avoid their duties in this field. Although there are organisational problems to be ironed out, and much modification is still necessary, there are also benefits for the pupils which are acknowledged by most professionals, not least where home–school liaison is concerned. Hopefully by the time the National Curriculum is fully implemented, much of the unnecessary paperwork and curriculum overload will be trimmed away, leaving a useful framework to support the professionals in doing the job they know best – educating young people according to their 'age, ability and aptitude'.

Glossary of terms

AT:	Attainment Target
DES:	Department of Education and Science
ERA:	Education Reform Act
INSET:	In-service Education of Teachers
LEA:	Local Education Authority
LMS:	Local Management of Schools
KS:	Key Stage
NAT:	New Attainment Target
NC:	National Curriculum
NCC:	National Curriculum Council
NSG:	Non-Statutory Guidance
PC:	Profile Component
PoS:	Programme of Study
RE:	Religious Education
RoA:	Records of Achievement
SACRE:	Standing Advisory Council on Religious Education
SAT:	Standard Assessment Task
SEAC:	School Examinations and Assessment Council
SoA:	Statement of Attainment
TA:	Teacher Assessment
TGAT:	Task Group on Assessment and Testing
WO:	Welsh Office

Further reading

Brighouse, T. and Moon, B. (eds.) (1990) *Managing the National Curriculum – Some Critical Perspectives*, Longman/BEMAS, Harlow.

Kelly, A.V. (1990) *The National Curriculum – A Critical Review*, Paul Chapman Publishing, London.

Merttens, R. and Vass, J. (1989) *The National Curriculum – A Survival Guide for Parents*, Octopus Publishing Group, Rushden, Northants.

Department of Education and Science/Welsh Office (DES/WO) (1988) *The Education Reform Act*, HMSO, London.

DES/WO (1989a) *English in the National Curriculum*, HMSO, London.

DES/WO (1989b) *Mathematics in the National Curriculum*, HMSO, London.

DES/WO (1989c) *Science in the National Curriculum*, HMSO, London.

DES/WO (1991a) *History in the National Curriculum*, HMSO, London.

DES/WO (1991b) *New Proposals for Mathematics and Science*, HMSO, London.

DES/WO (1991c) *Standard Assessment Task Teacher's Pack*, HMSO, London.

School Examination and Assessment Council (SEAC) (1990) *Records of Achievement in Primary Schools*, HMSO, London.

(Documents are also available for other foundation subjects. These are obtainable from schools, libraries and HMSO bookshops).

SECTION III

BECOMING AN EARLY YEARS TEACHER

7

TRAINING TO TEACH

Introduction

Opting to train as an infant teacher is never a decision that should be taken lightly: the courses are demanding, the hours long, the experience of teaching practice can be very traumatic and the workload from the moment you enter the college doors until you retire is never-ending! It is certainly not a profession which suits everyone but, as you will discover in the next section, it can be appropriate for young and old, males and females alike.

If you have read the book thus far you are obviously fairly enthusiastic and will have developed some impressions of the trials and tribulations of teaching. If, on the other hand, you have simply flicked through the pages until you have found a section which you hope will tell you how to apply for a course: think again! Are you prepared to read this – or any other book – on early years education prior to embarking on teacher training? If you are, fine. Of course it might make you change your mind about your chosen career but surely it is better sooner than later? More optimistically it might provide you with valuable insight which should, almost certainly, help you as you prepare for your future. Those of you who do not plan to read this or any such book for whatever reason should very seriously think again: you may claim to lack the time but it is *your* future at stake! You may claim you cannot afford to buy books but there are numerous public libraries to hand, the vast majority of which will include some basic texts on education. You may claim all sorts of other excuses: all I ask of you is to think.

Choosing the appropriate route to becoming a teacher is not usually straightforward and in this chapter I shall discuss some of the factors you should consider and explain your way forward. Throughout the chapter there are comments made by students attending a course at the University of East Anglia which, I hope, should provide a valuable perspective.

Although they were all undertaking a Postgraduate Certificate in Education (as opposed to any other course) I am not aware that the information given is particularly biased in that direction.

What sort of people opt for infant teaching?

The experience and age range of any group of student teachers tends to be vast. This year our students have come from many walks of life: some came straight through the education system (e.g. school, a degree and then our course); several had travelled extensively; quite a number had brought up families; there were two nurses, some social workers and a couple of librarians to name but a few. A minority were in their early twenties having come straight from university but the average age was 27 years old and many were in their thirties and forties.

On many courses selectors try to obtain a balance of students across a fairly broad age range. There are several reasons for this but, however old you are, it is important to appreciate that there are likely to be advantages and disadvantages of embarking on teacher training at your age! For example younger students tend to have more energy and are familiar with the forms of assessment used on many training courses (essays, projects etc.). However, 28-year-old Marianne, 'wouldn't recommend coming straight from university as I feel to go into teaching you need a lot of life experience.' Certainly older students can offer a variety of invaluable skills acquired while raising their children, travelling or working in another profession. On the other hand they sometimes find it harder adjusting to the demands of assignment writing and coping with the constructive criticism which accompanies any worthwhile form of assessment.

Finally, contrary to popular belief, it is not only females who train to become infant teachers! It is true that very few males contemplate embarking on a career in early years education but there is absolutely no reason why they should not. It is, after all, a very challenging and rewarding job which requires the energy, intelligence, sensitivity and insight of human beings rather than any peculiarly masculine or feminine skills. Having said that, male students tend to perceive their gender as 'an asset as it should help me get a job'! It is hard to say whether this is in fact the case because the males on our course tend to be very high calibre individuals and therefore, although they appear to have little difficulty in finding jobs, I suspect it is due to their personal and professional qualities rather than their gender.

Usually 5–10% of the students on our early years course are male. Apart from a seminar focusing on potential dilemmas for a male working with young children (e.g. how should you respond if a little girl wants to sit on your knee?), all our students follow the same course regardless of their gender.

Finding out about teaching?

Having decided to pursue a career in infant teaching the very first thing you should do is go and spend some time working with young children *in a school setting*. This is crucial because – however vivid your imagination – the occasional night babysitting is a far cry from educating thirty young children all day every day.

Setting up some time in a school should be quite straightforward as the majority of schools are used to visitors and welcome an extra pair of hands! Some careers offices have an arrangement with a local school and, if you contact them, can organise a visit for you. Alternatively, simply look under 'schools' in the yellow pages of the telephone directory and select the most convenient first, primary or infant school in your area. Ring the school and ask to speak to the headteacher. Explain that you are thinking about training to become a teacher and would like to observe and assist in some early years' classrooms for a week (or however much time you can spare). I would be surprised if your offer was refused but, if it is, do not be put off: some schools are so overrun with visitors that, from time to time, they simply have to say, 'No more!'

Assuming that the school is happy to have you, arrange a mutually convenient time to begin your placement there. At the risk of sounding condescending, two tips which may seem trivial but which can make quite a difference: dress the part and arrive in good time. By dressing the part I mean wear smart but sensible clothes which will cast you in the role of a professional who is prepared to be splattered in paint! Arriving in plenty of time is not only a courtesy but it is an essential habit for a teacher (you daren't leave thirty 4-year-olds waiting after all). Furthermore it creates a good impression which may be useful should you need a reference at a later date.

What happens next depends on the school but, ideally, you should acquire a flavour of the job by helping out where required; visiting a range of classes; talking to people and observing everyone and everything! (See Chapter 2 for the appropriate techniques). If at all possible, repeat the experience at another school because – as you will discover – schools, teachers and pupils can be markedly different from one another.

The value of spending time in a school prior to applying to a course cannot be underestimated for, as several of our students discovered, they were not fully aware of the demands of the job until they observed practitioners close at hand and tried teaching for themselves:

'I didn't realise it would be such hard work.'
'It's a lot harder and more stressful than I expected. Your attention is on the job the whole time. You can't afford to switch off as in an office.'
'I didn't realise how much time preparation actually took.'
'I didn't realise it involved so much academic work and writing reports . . . Teachers are constantly giving out of themselves though they do get a lot back.'
'I have been impressed by some teachers who have been more reflective and probing than I expected.'

Having decided to embark on a career in teaching the next step is to find out about the various courses available to you (see below), send off for prospectuses. Some of these may appear very attractive and immediately grab your attention but do not be misled: it may be that further examination reveals very little relevant content. Other prospectuses may be rather dull in appearance (colourful covers cost money) but be crammed full of useful information: how much contact will you have with children? What range of courses will there be? Is there anyone particularly eminent on the staff? Etc.

Finally – and most importantly – I urge you to ask as many teachers as possible about how and where they trained. Some of what they say may be dated but it should certainly give you some insight into what you might be letting yourself in for.

Choosing your training route

Teacher education is in a time of rapid change. What is written today might well be out of date by the time you read this and therefore it is crucial that you thoroughly research what options are currently available to you as you contemplate entering the teaching profession. A good starting point is to contact your local careers office. Alternatively you could write to the Department of Education and Science in London, TEACH in Edinburgh, or the Northern Ireland Education Office. (The addresses are given at the end of this chapter.)

Broadly speaking, at the time of writing, there are three routes into teaching. The first is to embark on an undergraduate degree leading to a teaching qualification. These are available at universities, colleges of higher education or polytechnics. They are generally four year courses which provide you with a Bachelor of Arts (B.A.) or a Bachelor of Education (B.Ed.). Applications for such courses should be made through UCCA. The address is given at the end of the chapter.

If, on leaving school, you are uncertain about your choice of career you would be wiser to select the second option: namely do a degree in something that particularly interests you and then either enrol on a one year Postgraduate Certificate of Education (PGCE) course or undertake two years as an articled teacher. Both courses require similar entry requirements. A word of warning however, your choice of degree subject *may* limit the number of courses for which you may enrol. For example, *some* institutions will only accept graduates in subjects traditionally taught in school. Thus, if you have a good mathematics degree you are likely to be invited for interview but your chances would be dramatically reduced if your degree were in sociology. That does not mean to say that the profession is devoid of highly proficient infant teachers with sociology degrees!

Polytechnics, colleges of higher education and universities throughout the country run PGCE courses. They usually run full time for thirty-six weeks and are currently the most common form of entry into the profession for graduates. As will be discussed below, most people on such courses are eligible for grants. For further details of courses in England and Wales refer to *The Handbook of Initial Teacher Training* which is produced every year and which should be available in your local library or careers centre. Application forms and other relevant information are available from the Graduate Teacher Training Registry (GTTR). (The address is at the end of the chapter.) Details of PGCE courses in Scotland are outlined in the *Memorandum of Entry Requirements of Courses of Teacher Training in Scotland* which is published yearly by the Scottish Education Department. Application forms may be obtained from the individual institutions or from TEACH. (Details at the end of the chapter.) Information on courses in Northern Ireland should be available at your local careers centre. Applications for these courses should be made directly to the institutions of your choice.

Articled teacher courses began in 1990 and are open to graduates. They are two years in duration and – unlike many PGCE courses – are largely school-based throughout this time. Bursaries – which are worth considerably more than a grant – are available for suitably qualified individuals. Further particulars and application forms for such courses may be obtained from the GTTR (address at the end of the chapter).

Finally, in recent years the government have proposed on-the-job training schemes such as licensed teaching. These schemes are still in their infancy but it may be worth exploring such possibilities before committing yourself to a particular form of training. At the time of writing, to qualify for a licensed teacher scheme you need to be at least 26 years old and have successfully completed the equivalent of two years full-time higher education in the UK or elsewhere and have attained Grade C in GCSE Mathematics and English or the equivalent. Refer to your local careers centre or the Department of Education and Science (address below) for further details.

Selecting where to train

On what criteria should you base your decision? Within each type of training – be it a B.Ed., PGCE or whatever – there is quite a variation in what is on offer. To a certain extent the government have dictated minimum requirements (e.g. 4-year B.Ed. courses must include at least 100 days of school experience). Nevertheless there is still considerable flexibility and it is wise to investigate courses from a range of institutions. For example will you have to do exams at some places and not others? What is the balance between theoretical and practical work (see below)? Are there any specialist options on offer?

For some the selection process is straightforward. As Sheila explains, 'This course was nearest me. In fact I didn't have a choice as I couldn't afford to move.' Mary simply said, 'I had to be in Norwich'.

For others the type of training is important. On and off since the time of pupil-teachers there have been suggestions for on-the-job training. There are certain advantages to such an approach: you are paid more than a grant (see below) as you train; you tend to be settled in the same school as you train and you receive plenty of 'hands-on' experience. By some it is seen as a dive in at the deep end and a sink or swim approach to teaching. If you should opt for such a scheme ensure that you have a range of people to call on for support. It may be, for example, that you do not feel at ease with your 'mentor' (guiding teacher tutor) and feel happier discussing your work with someone else.

As mentioned above, if you opt for an on-the-job training scheme you are likely to do most – if not all – your training in one school but, as Paul explains, one disadvantage of such a system is the likelihood that, 'It would give you a very limited view of what goes on in the classroom.' More specifically, schools vary enormously and it is important that you observe – and work in – a variety of situations so that you can experience a range of possible approaches to early years education. Even more fundamentally, Jo made the point that she would not undertake on-the-job training as, 'It perpetuates the system as it is. I wanted to know how it could be done and get a spread of views'.

Jo's remark in the previous paragraph also illustrates the need for a balance in the practical and theoretical input on the course you select. When they start their training the majority of students eagerly await 'tips for teachers'. They view teaching in much the same way as driving a car: tell me which key to turn and which pedal to press and I will be all set to go. As you will soon discover, teaching is very far from being as simple as that. There are certain skills that you can acquire when engaged in practical work such as how to use your voice effectively. But tips can only really equip you for a limited range of situations.

After struggling to teach 5-year-old Jason to count, for example, Sophie attended a lecture on the development of counting skills. The lecturer explained that there are several important concepts which a child needs to understand before they will be able to count items in the conventional way (e.g. sorting, matching and ordering). As the session proceeded Sophie began to appreciate that Jason did indeed have some of the prerequisite skills necessary for counting but that he still had not mastered the stable order principle which requires a person to appreciate that the labels we use for counting (i.e. these are generally numbers) must always be recited in the same order. Jason, on the other hand, had been 'counting' by saying 'one, two, nine, six', for example, one minute and then 'one, four, three, eight' the next. Over the next few weeks Sophie applied this knowledge of the development of counting skills by giving Jason plenty of practice in reciting number poems and songs and by demonstrating her own counting whenever she could (e.g. doing the register, counting out pencils, organising teams in PE). She later explained:

> To be honest, before I came to college I really had very little time for anything other than work in the classroom but I found that the theory gave me a far greater understanding of how children learn to count. At the beginning of the practice I had seen the teacher counting the names on the register but I thought that she was just doing it to check how many children were at school. I guess I thought that learning to count was confined to maths sessions. When I learnt about the theories of learning in general, and counting in particular, I really began to appreciate the need for a theoretical underpinning in my classroom-based work. I now feel far more confident about teaching children how to count effectively.

Most initial training courses involve studying with other student teachers. For a variety of reasons this is generally perceived as an advantage. Such contact provides another source of information and experience.

'You get ideas from each other.'
'I've enjoyed working with others as everyone has come with lots of different experiences and there is a wide age range.'
'Talking things through helps you understand.'

Working with others can also provide emotional support when faced with the pressures of teaching practice or essay writing.

'It's nice to have someone in the same position as you as they have the same worries.'
'You can share camaraderie and you are in similar positions to each other.'

Jo remarked that, 'Contact with others gives you moral support' but added that being in a group can be difficult sometimes. She explained, 'I found the February depression very catching so I had very much to keep my own aims in mind.' Similarly Susie liked being with others as, 'you can discuss things with each other' but she pointed out that: 'It sometimes makes me feel that they are doing a wonderful job and I'm not'.

Some courses involve two students working together in the same classroom on their first teaching practice. Inevitably this can lead to the comparisons Susie described above but, more generally, students tend to view it as a positive and helpful experience.

'I liked having a student with me on first teaching practice as you can share experience.'
'We've learnt a lot from each other especially in the first term having someone else in the classroom.'

Although the above criteria for selecting your course are all relevant perhaps even more important is the financing of it. Before you submit an application for a training course you should explore how you will finance it and whether you would be eligible for a grant. This will be considered in the next section.

In brief, some courses will be more suited to your needs than others. You may have little choice in where you go if you are late in applying or are confined to a specific area but, nevertheless, you would be wise to find out as much as you can about a course before you apply for it so that you can make optimum use of your time in training.

Financing your training

If you opt for an initial teacher training course or a postgraduate certificate in education course you will almost certainly be eligible for a grant if certain conditions are met. For example, in most cases candidates must have been resident in the UK for three years before 1 September of the year in which their course begins; your chances will be reduced if you have received a grant for similiar professional courses (e.g. if you have already trained as a social worker) in the past and so on. For further information write to the Department of Education and Science requesting copies of *Grants for Students: a brief guide* and *Loans for Students: a brief guide*. The address is given at the end of this chapter.

Articled teachers are generally eligible for a bursary and should apply to the Local Education Authority in whose schools they are studying.

If you are applying for an on-the-job training scheme, such as licensed teaching, establish your salary with the school before committing yourself as it may be considerably less than you imagine.

Applying for a course

Once you have selected the course(s) you wish to apply for you will need to complete the relevant application form(s). These may be obtained from UCCA, the GTTR, TEACH or, in the case of Northern Ireland, from the individual institutions. Addresses are given at the end of this chapter.

Over the years it has become apparent to me that some candidates simply do not appreciate that, initially, their application form is the sum total of all the information that I have about them. Personally, I do struggle my way through all the applications that land on my desk but, I can assure you, the ones that are well laid out and neatly presented put me in a far better mood than those that are illegible and scruffy and that is before I discover the content! There is no doubt about it, filling in application forms properly takes time but, if you are serious in your intentions, it should be worth the effort.

Ideally, make – and complete – a photocopy of the application form when you receive it. That should reduce the chances of you falling into the trap that I almost invariably do i.e. not reading the entire form at the outset and completing question (1) in such detail that I also manage to complete questions (2), (3) and (4) in the process! A trial run through of the form also provides you with opportunities to clarify your thinking and *to check your spelling*. It may sound trivial but a badly spelt application form can create the impression that the applicant is 'unintieligent and lazie'. If poss- ible, ask a friend to read through your answers before you complete the final version stressing that she should check for errors and consider whether you have managed to convey an accurate – but complimentary –

picture of yourself. For example, if you have worked with children say so outlining the responsibilities you were given.

At the end of your form you are likely to be asked to nominate two referees. Usually one of these should be someone who knows you academically and the other someone (not a relative) who knows you as an individual. *Please* ask your referees if they are willing to act on your behalf *before* submitting their names. There are two very good reasons for this. The first is that it is sheer good manners and is likely to put you in a better light. The other is that, by the warmth of your proposed referee's response, you may gain an impression of the quality of the reference they might write for you. If they refuse or do not appear very keen you would be wise to seek someone else.

Having done a draft, the actual application form should be fairly easy to complete. Opinion is divided but, unless it is otherwise stated, write – rather than type – your application. Write as legibly as possible using black ink as the form will undoubtedly be photocopied. If you are unlucky enough to make a mistake I would recommend using tippex or the equivalent but, failing that, cross out your error as neatly as possible and try not to make any more! Finally retain a copy of your application so that you may refer to it in preparation for your interview.

Unless asked to do so, there is no need to include a curriculum vitae with your application form.

The selection interview

If you are invited for an interview remember that it is not simply an opportunity for 'them' to select you but also for *you* to select 'them'. That you might argue, is all very well for someone with a job to say and, in some ways, you are right but let me give you an example. Several years ago I went for a job interview. It began with a tour round the campus which looked pleasant enough although the atmosphere was rather sterile: the walls were bare and everyone looked highly efficient and smart. There was not a genuine smile to be seen. The actual interview was extremely formal with about six besuited people on one side of a huge table and me on the other side. Unlike some interviews I have been to I had no real difficulty in answering any of the questions posed. Nevertheless I came away feeling uneasy. It was undoubtedly a well run institution but the whole place seemed to be full of automatons. There was no enthusiasm, sincerity or interest in people. They were not even courteous enough at the end of the interview to ask whether I had any questions of my own. If I had been offered the post I would have been in a real dilemma. Fortunately I was first reserve so honour was maintained but I never really had to confront the idea of working in an unhappy, soulless environment.

So what should you be looking for when you go along for an interview? That, to some extent, depends on you but I think two basic questions you must ask yourself are: 'Do I want to spend any time here? Can these people provide a course that I'll be happy with?' Answers to these questions may be obtained by observing how you are treated: do you feel welcomed, for example? Do people smile at you as they pass you in the corridor? Do the interviewers appear to listen to you? Are you shown round? Are you given an opportunity to ask any questions? (A word of warning here: as an interviewer I am more than happy if candidates ask questions about our course and the teaching profession. I am not, however, overly impressed if the questions demonstrate that the candidate has clearly not read our prospectus!)

If you can, you might find it useful to read a copy of the course handbook which is currently being used by students already attending the course. This should give you another perspective on the course for which you are applying and it might also provoke some questions. For example, are the aims of the course outlined? How do they compare to the list below?

The Postgraduate Certificate in Education (PGCE) is designed to initiate you into the systematic study of the theory and practice of teaching in the 4–8-year age range and to translate this knowledge into your own classroom practice. It is seen as the beginning of a lifelong learning experience.

More specifically, the programme is intended to enable you to:

(1) Acquire knowledge and understanding of young children's affective, cognitive and physical development and behaviour.
(2) Master a basic knowledge and understanding of the main areas of the early years curriculum and to prepare you for a subject specialism.
(3) Create an environment that will facilitate children's cognitive, affective and social development.
(4) Reflect on your own practice and modify your teaching strategies and professional attitudes as appropriate.
(5) Develop your interpersonal skills so that you may share your professional experiences and respect other points of view.
(6) Be adaptable in the face of a changing educational system.
(7) Evolve your own educational philosophy.
(8) Develop a concern for wider educational issues and consider their implications for society and the classroom.

(Early Years Team, 1990, p. 3)

And what are the interviewers looking for? The Council for the Accreditation of Teacher Education (CATE) has laid down some guidelines for the selection of student teachers. For example, in addition to the formal qualifications (i.e. necessary examination grades etc.) the CATE Committee advise teacher educators that

> An assessment of personal qualities is particularly important when selecting intending teachers since their ability to teach and manage classes depends on the relationships they form with children and their teacher colleagues. The personal qualities which selection procedures are designed to explore should include: a sense of responsibility; a robust but balanced outlook; the potential ability to relate well to children; sensitivity; enthusiasm and a facility for communicating.
>
> (Department of Education and Science, 1989, p. 21)

How can you convey that you have the above qualities? By being well prepared; by appearing to take the interview seriously but demonstrating a sense of humour; by being yourself. More specifically, you should do some background reading about the profession (by reading this book!); be prepared to express your own opinions about topical educational issues (currently these include the National Curriculum and assessment) and show that you know something about the course you are applying for. You should not, in my view, arrive in jeans and a crumpled tee-shirt (some people do!) but do not feel that you have to break the bank to buy an outfit for the day: a clean, well pressed and relatively smart outfit will do (i.e. probably a skirt or dress for females and a jacket and tie for males).

And, as I said, be yourself. Don't worry if you are nervous. That is natural and any good interviewers will take that into account. They will not be trying to catch you out but simply ascertaining whether you are likely to make a good teacher of young children. They will soon spot if you are trying to be something you are not. And if, in their opinion you are not cut out to be a teacher, isn't it better to discover that early on than several weeks into a course or, worse still, during your final teaching practice?

Finally, if it is some time since you have had an interview or if you feel particularly anxious or inexperienced, I suggest you go along to a careers office as they should be able to give advice on the matter and may even offer you a mock interview.

Dropping out

There is absolutely no doubt about it: training to be an infant teacher is hard work! It would be misleading to suggest that everyone thrives on it and passes with flying colours. But rest assured. If you are committed, have been accepted on to a course which is oversubscribed having undergone a rigorous interview and made all the necessary preparations, then all should be well. For example, this year our intake was forty-five early years PGCE (postgraduate certificate in education) students and only one of them decided that the job was not for her when she discovered the realities of teaching.

It is important to recognise, however, that during your training some individuals – and possibly even you – may contemplate abandoning the course. This usually occurs when energy levels are low and the demands of the course seem particularly high. Not infrequently this occurs around February which is generally accepted as a period of low morale in many walks of life. Jo explains when she hit a low ebb:

> I did think of leaving but it was largely through illness, sick children and a poor first teaching practice plus the problems of being a single parent.

Jo quickly overcame these problems, 'Knowing I wanted to teach was enough.' Far more common responses to the question: 'Have you ever thought of leaving the course?' ranged from 'No' to an emphatic 'No, definitely not!' Mary believed, 'It's too important' and Anna was adamant that, 'The only way that I'd leave the course is if I fail.'

The assessment of practical teaching

Whatever form of teaching you decide upon, at some time you will have another adult assessing your capabilities as a teacher. Perhaps contrary to your expectations, this does not only refer to your teaching performance but includes, among other things, how you prepare your work, how you interact with the school staff, how you relate to children and their parents in non-teaching situations and the quality of your classroom wall display.

It is natural to find the idea of such visits nerve-racking initially. I was absolutely terrified! But, as Marianne explains, 'It's a bit like a driving test at first. I was shaking on the first visit. But it gets better. On the whole the comments have been very helpful.'

Some students (often the older ones) find it hard to accept criticism and, like Anna, it can take several visits for them to recognise the value of a constructive evaluation of their progress:

> I now know it is necessary for the teaching process . . . I realise that I am not here to get it right but to learn how to teach. I hadn't really appreciated that.

The most successful students tend to have a very positive view of assessment:

> 'I don't find it a problem. It's necessary and it's useful. I see it as very constructive.'
> 'I don't mind being assessed. It's really helpful pointing out where to go and what you should be looking at.'
> 'When you are teaching you can't always see what is wrong yourself and therefore it is good to have someone point it out to you.'

On occasion students comment that tutors have not been critical enough! Susie remarked:

> I felt she was too generous, to be honest. I'd prefer a bit more criticism.

In other words, from the moment you first walk into the classroom it is important to remember that no one – including yourself – should expect a perfect performance. A union pamphlet states:

> Many students place too high an expectation upon their initial performance and are disillusioned and discouraged. You should, of course, aim

to excel but you should not be disappointed if your limited experience does not permit you to match the performance of more experienced teachers around you in the school. The purpose of teaching practice is to enable you to develop your teaching skills in as realistic an environment as possible. It is inevitable that some mistakes will be made but the most important thing is that the lesson of such errors is properly learned.

(NASUWT and NUS, 1989, p. 3)

In addition, you should be aware that, in most cases, your assessor's role will not simply be to evaluate but also to provide you with some practical and emotional support. To a large extent this is because training to be a teacher can be very demanding. However, it should be recognised that, occasionally students find themselves in schools that are less than sympathetic to their needs. For example Jo 'found it very difficult to follow the headteacher's philosophy'. Obviously, ideally, all students would be placed in perfect schools but, with the best will in the world, this is simply not possible. And, as Mary sums it up:

The whole thing of teaching practice is difficult because the schools vary so much: the staff, the children, the resources.

Other forms of assessment

Without a doubt, whatever training you decide upon there will be some type of additional assessment. In the past this has tended to be in the form of examinations but, increasingly, continuous assessment has taken over. This usually entails written assignments, dissertations, projects or a combination of these. Irrespective of age and experience clearly some individuals find such work unappealing:

I don't like essays. I don't see why we should write the essays. There is no point in the assessment at all.

Often older students are anxious about writing their first assignment:

'I found it quite difficult as I haven't written an essay since my degree ten years ago.'
'I was quite frightened about doing it.'

But, as Sheila points out, such written work can be a valuable exercise:

I've never liked writing essays but I don't think they are a waste of time. I have learnt something from each of them. The second assignment made my aims and objectives clearer. It also helped me plan my work.

Others also found essay writing useful:

> 'They have helped me matching work to children.'
> 'The essays help you review what you have done.'
> 'They've all helped me think about and reflect on what I've done.'

Whatever form your assignments take they will probably be assessed and, in all likelihood, returned with some constructive criticism. Do not be down-hearted! Remember you are not an expert and that your training should be seen as the beginning of a life-long learning experience.

In essence the more positively and constructively you view all forms of assessment, the more you will gain from them.

Conclusion

Training to become a teacher of young children is not an easy option and you should endeavour to ensure that that is your chosen option before you embark on it. Choose your course with care bearing in mind any financial, domestic or other restrictions which might limit your choice. You will have doubts throughout your training and subsequent career but remember Cathy's words towards the end of the fourth chapter:

> I find that children and their learning are so fascinating that I would not want to be anywhere else.

A checklist of questions

- Is teaching for you?
- Which course best suits your qualifications, aspirations and situation?
- Can you finance your training?
- Have you completed your application form in a professional manner?
- Are you fully prepared for your interview?
- Do you like the people and place where you plan to train?

Some useful addresses

If you are thinking of doing an undergraduate teacher training course write to:

UCCA,
P.O. Box 28,
Cheltenham
GL50 1HY

For entry to postgraduate and articled teacher courses in England and Wales contact:

The Graduate Teacher Training Registry (GTTR),
P.O. Box 239,
Cheltenham
GL 50 3SL

Another useful address where you can obtain more general information and details about grants is:

TASC (Teaching as a career)
The Department of Education and Science,
Elizabeth House,
York Road,
London
SE1 7PH

For information on teacher training courses in Scotland or Northern Ireland you should write to:

Teacher Education Admissions
Clearing House (TEACH),
PO Box 165,
Edinburgh
EH8 8AT

Northern Ireland Education Office,
Rathgael House,
Balloo Road,
Bangor
BT19 2PR

Further reading

For more general information I suggest that you read the following publications:

Graduate Teacher Training Registry (yearly) *Course Entry: Guide for applicants*, Cheltenham, GTTR.

National Association of Teachers of Further and Higher Education (yearly) *The Handbook of Initial Teacher Training*. London, NATFHE.

Scottish Education Department (yearly) *Memorandum on Entry Requirements for Admission to Courses of Teacher Training in Scotland*, HMSO, Edinburgh.

SECTION IV

THOUGHTS FOR THE FUTURE

8
CONCLUDING REMARKS

> He who undertakes the education of a child undertakes the most import-
> ant duty of society.
>
> Thomas Day (1748–89)

The education system in Great Britain today is in a time of rapid change.
We are currently being inundated with new curricula, new assessment
arrangements, new organisational and management policies, to name but
some. It has been argued, however, that external decisions usually have
very little fundamental effect on classroom practice (Cockburn, 1986). On
reflection, this is not so surprising for Greeno (1980) observed that

> the nature of the concepts and skills to be acquired (in school) has been
> shaped by a process of evolution in which materials that cannot be
> learned by most students (i.e. pupils) and methods of instruction that
> have been patently unsuccessful have been eliminated over the years.
>
> (p. 726) (brackets added)

It is also interesting to note that many of today's principles of early childhood education discussed in Chapter 3 were derived from the Ancient
Greeks. Moreover you will find that William James' book written almost
100 years ago (1899) still provides many relevant and practical ideas for the
modern infant classroom.

This is not to say that formal schooling neither can – nor will – ever
change other than superficially. Indeed Charles Desforges (currently a
professor at Exeter University) likens this period to the years immediately
before the Wright brothers in aviation history. Their predecessors wanted
to fly and so looked to birds for the secret. Unfortunately this approach was

doomed to failure and merely led to a lot of flapping about on the ground (the power/weight ratio of a bird being inappropriate for a machine). It took the Wright brothers' totally revolutionary ideas to lift us into the air. It could be that such a reconceptualisation may soon be upon us in the educational world. A serious discussion of this idea is beyond the scope of this book but it is a tantalising thought and it will be most interesting to see what happens over the next decade or so.

But, whatever the future of schooling in this country there is no doubt about it, should you decide to become an infant teacher you will be entering one of the most rewarding, interesting and demanding professions. For me it is rather like doing my doctorate: hard work, absorbing, challenging and never far from my thoughts from the moment I embarked on the enterprise. (I am told that motherhood is just the same only more so!)

If you have the right qualifications and personal qualities, your chances of gaining a place on a course are reasonably high assuming that you apply in plenty of time and prepare yourself well (see Chapter 7). Thereafter, assuming you perform satisfactorily, your chances of gaining a job are likely to be very good although this probability fluctuates with the birth rate and varies from area to area. For example, if the birth rate four or five years earlier was low and you plan to work in a poorly populated area where there are several training establishments, your chances of finding a job will be less than if you apply for a post in Central London where there always seem to be plenty of vacancies.

Even if all goes smoothly – you are accepted on a course, pass with flying colours and get a first rate job – let me warn you that it will not all be enjoyable and straightforward. Apart from the sheer hard work you will find yourself under numerous pressures from all sides: for example, from pupils' parents, from your colleagues and headteacher, from the government, from yourself and last – but by no means least – from the children themselves. For, whatever we would like to believe, let's face it: pupils of even the most outstanding teachers are not all perfect all of the time. There is no doubt about it: all children can be awkward from time to time but – with experience and skill – a good teacher can usually anticipate and defuse potentially difficult situations.

Moreover, as you will discover, the actions of children make some types of session (e.g. where the children complete familiar worksheets) generally easier to manage, but of less educational value, than others (e.g. discussions). Having had experience of a variety of approaches you might find it interesting to read books such as *Understanding the Mathematics Teacher: a study of practice in first schools* (Desforges and Cockburn, 1987) for you will begin to appreciate why some of the more meaningful forms of education are often more difficult to effect than others.

Before I move on, let me draw your attention to an earlier suggestion that, among other things, you might also experience pressure from yourself. If you are any good as a teacher this will undoubtedly be true and it is certainly no bad thing for you to strive to maintain your standards. The danger lies in the fact that you may be unrealistic in setting your goals and you may be ruthless in your pursuit of them. If you wish to be a successful teacher you must strike a balance and remember that there is life beyond the classroom: totally dedicated teachers are not only generally rather dull but they tend to be unfulfilled as human beings. Of course you will need to work hard but, take my advice, pursue a hobby or two and – dare I suggest – even take a Saturday or Sunday off now and again!

So far in this chapter I have been describing situations where all has gone relatively smoothly in your training and subsequent employment. You may be unlucky enough, however, to find yourself in a school which you really dislike and where you seem to be making little, if any, progress. Nothing seems to go right and the staff are constantly criticising you and putting you down. Sadly, despite care in selecting schools for teaching practice, this can happen during your training and, despite careful research on your part, it could happen on your first appointment. It may be that infant teaching is really not for you but do not give up without thought and discussion with others. There will always be someone sympathetic with whom you can discuss the matter. For example it may be a tutor from your college, a teacher or an adviser from the Local Education Authority. You may like to talk to another student about it but, if you do, remember that they may not possess the necessary objectivity and experience to advise you appropriately. Remember too that, whatever we would like to imagine, not all schools are perfect. If you are on teaching practice you may be able to transfer to a more suitable school under exceptional circumstances but, more likely, you may have to stay where you are for the time being. If nothing else you will pick up what not to do and, who knows, you may even go a little way towards improving a less than ideal school.

Sadly, such schools tend to give teachers and teaching a bad name. Hardly a day goes by without there being some article or other criticising the profession. Many people like to have someone or something to complain about and, seemingly, headlines such as: 'My 10-year-old can't read' or 'Spelling standards drop', make good press.

Do not be misled! The vast majority of teachers are doing an excellent job. I have seen numerous individuals educating young children and it would be true to say that nine out of every ten of them are doing it in a highly professional, conscientious and competent manner. You may argue that I lack objectivity and thrust a report under my nose 'proving' that – for example – reading standards have fallen. But such material needs to be analysed with care and should not be read in isolation. More specifically, the problems involved in measuring standards at any given time are exceedingly complex and tax even the most knowledgeable. Let me explain two of the reasons why this is so.

The first is that if you wish to assess standards in, say, language at two different times it is only fair that you use the same test to make the assessment both times (otherwise you would always be left with the query, 'Did I measure exactly the same things?') But, if you use a test which was considered ideal in 1970, you will find that it is likely to be outdated and not entirely appropriate for modern usage: the meanings of some of the words used may have changed slightly; the grammar may be slightly different and even the pictures might look old-fashioned. Take a look!

The second point about assessing standards is that it is unlikely that you are making a fair comparison when comparing one situation and moment in time with another. Take, for example, the case of science in first schools: twenty years ago there was virtually no science – other than nature studies – in early years classrooms and so pupils' knowledge of the subject was extremely limited. With the coming of the National Curriculum there has been a dramatic increase in the amount of science being studied by young children and therefore it is highly probable that standards will have risen. Taking the argument further you may begin to ponder, 'If there is an increase in science, where has there been a decrease?' As yet this is not altogether clear but, nevertheless, you may wonder: 'Is it fair to compare pupils who spent seven hours a week doing something ten years ago with those who only spend four hours a week on it now?' Many are unaware of such an argument but are only too ready to criticise teachers and the educational system, bringing me to my next point.

In the eyes of the uninformed, teachers and teaching still retain a fairly low status but this is changing as the profession becomes increasingly more accountable and more accessible to the general population. For example, parents now have a right to learn about – and become involved in – their children's education. The mystique is gradually being removed as parents and teachers come to trust and respect one another. Thus the profession is gradually gaining the esteem it so richly deserves but which, in the past, has only been articulated by a minority.

To conclude, this is an exciting and challenging time to be entering the teaching profession. By becoming a teacher you will become part of a profession beginning to realise its potential. You will have the chance to

fulfil your own potential. And you will be given the opportunity to help generations of young children discover and achieve their potential. It will not be easy but, I can assure you, it will almost certainly be rewarding and worthwhile.

Further reading

Cockburn, A.D. (1986) An Empirical Study of Classroom Processes in Infant Mathematics Education, unpublished doctoral thesis, University of East Anglia.

Desforges, C.W. (1990) Unpublished Master of Arts Seminar, University of East Anglia, November.

Desforges, C.W. and Cockburn, A.D. (1987) *Understanding the Mathematics Teacher: a study of practice in first schools*, Falmer Press, Lewes.

Greeno, J.C. (1980) Psychology of learning 1960–1980: One participant's observations, *American Psychologist*, 35, 713–728.

James, W. (1899) *Talks to Teachers*, Longmans, Green and Company Ltd, London.

REFERENCES

Anning, A. (1991) *The First Years at School*, Open University Press, Milton Keynes.

Axline, V.M., (1964) *Dibs: In Search of Self*, Penguin Books, London.

Brighouse, T. and Moon, B. (eds.) (1990) *Managing the National Curriculum — Some Critical Perspectives*. Longman/BEMAS, Harlow.

Brown, G. (1986) *Child Development*, (2nd ed), Open Books, Wells.

Brown, M. and Precious, N. (1968) *The Integrated Day in the Primary School*, Ward Lock Educational, London.

Bruce, T. (1987) *Early Childhood Education*, Hodder & Stoughton, London.

Buxton, L. (1981) *Do You Panic About Maths?*, Heinemann, London.

Carle, E. (1970) *The Very Hungry Caterpillar*, Puffin Books, London.

Central Adivsory Committee for Education (1967) *Children and their Primary Schools*, vol. 1, (The Plowden Report), HMSO, London.

Chazan, M., Laing, A. and Harper, G. (1987) *Teaching Five to Eight Year Olds*. Blackwell, Oxford.

Cockburn, A.D. (1986) An empirical study of classroom processes in infant mathematics education, unpublished doctoral thesis, University of East Anglia.

Cockburn, A.D. (1988) Promoting mathematical understanding in the early years of schooling – is it possible? Paper presented at the Annual Conference of the American Educational Research Association, New Orleans, April.

Cohen, L. and Manion, L. (1977) *A Guide to Teaching Practice*, Methuen, London.

Davis, R. (1988) *Learning to Teach in the Primary School*, Hodder & Stoughton, London.

Department of Education and Science (1989) *Initial Teacher Training: Approval of Courses Circular 24/89*, DES, London.

Department of Education and Science and Welsh Office (DES/WO) (1988) *The Education Reform Act*, HMSO, London.

DES/WO (1989a) *English in the National Curriculum*, HMSO, London.

DES/WO (1989b) *Mathematics in the National Curriculum*, HMSO, London.

DES/WO (1989c) *Science in the National Curriculum*, HMSO, London.

DES/WO (1991a) *History in the National Curriculum*, HMSO, London.

DES/WO (1991b) *New Proposals for Mathematics and Science*, HMSO, London.

DES/WO (1991c) *Standard Assessment Task Teacher's Pack*, HMSO, London.

Desforges, C.W. (1990) Unpublished Master of Arts seminar, University of East Anglia, April.

Desforges, C.W. and Cockburn, A.D. (1987) *Understanding the Mathematics Teacher: a Study of Practice in First Schools*, Falmer Press, Lewes.

Donaldson, M. (1978) *Children's Minds*, Collins, Glasgow.

Donaldson, M., Grieve, R. and Pratt, C. (eds.) (1983) *Early Childhood Development and Education*, Blackwell, Oxford.

Early Years Team (1990), *PGCE Early Years Course: Student Handbook 1990–91*, Unpublished, University of East Anglia.

Fynn (1974) *Mister God this is Anna*, Collins, London.

Graduate Teacher Training Registry (yearly) *Course Entry: Guide for Applicants*, GTTR, Cheltenham.

Greeno, J.C. (1980) Psychology of learning 1960–1980: one participant's observations, *American Psychologist*, 35, 713–728

Hill, W.F. (1985) *Learning*, (4th edn), Harper and Row, New York.

Holt, J. (1964) *How Children Fail*, Penguin, Harmondsworth.

Howe, M.J.A. (1984) *Psychology of Learning*, Blackwell, Oxford.

Hughes, M. (1986) *Children and Number*, Blackwell, Oxford.

James, W. (1899) *Talks to Teachers*, Longmans, Green and Company Ltd., London.

Kelly, A.V. (1990) *The National Curriculum – A Critical Review*, Paul Chapman Publishing, London.

Laing, R.D. (1984) *Conversations with Adam and Natasha*, Pantheon Books, New York.

Manning, K. and Sharp, A. (1977) *Structuring Play in the Early Years*, Ward Lock Educational/Schools Council, London.

Merttens, R. and Vass, J. (1989) *The National Curriculum – A Survival Guide for Parents*, Octopus Publishing Group, Rushden, Northants.

Moyles, J.R. (1989) *Just Playing?*, Open University Press, Milton Keynes.

NASUWT and NUS (1989) *An Education Student's Guide to Teaching Practice*, National Union of Students Publication, London.

National Association of Teachers of Further and Higher Education (yearly) *The Handbook of Initial Training*, NATFHE, London.

National Curriculum Council (1989a) *English: Non-Statutory Guidance*, HMSO, London.

National Curriculum Council (1989b) *Mathematics: Non-Statutory Guidance*, HMSO, London.

National Curriculum Council (1989c) *Science: Non-Statutory Guidance*, HMSO, London.

Nuffield Mathematics Project (1967) *I do and I understand*, Chambers and Murray, London.

Paley, V.G. (1981) *Wally's Stories*, Harvard University Press, Cambridge, Mass.

Pollard, A. (1990) *Learning in Primary Schools*, Cassell, London,

School Examination and Assessment Council (1990) *Records of Achievement in Primary Schools*, HMSO, London.

Scottish Education Department (yearly) *Memorandum on Entry Requirements for Admission to Courses of Teacher Training in Scotland*, HMSO, Edinburgh.

Tizard, B. and Hughes, M. (1984) *Young Children Learning: Talking and Thinking at Home and at School*, Fontana, London.

Walker, R. and Adelman, C. (1975) *A Guide to Classroom Observation*, Methuen & Co. Ltd, London.

Ward, G. and Rowe, J. (1985) Teachers' praise: some unwanted side effects or 'praise and be damned', *Society for Extension of Education Knowledge*, Vol.1, pp 2–4.

ASSESSMENT IN EARLY CHILDHOOD EDUCATION

Edited by Geva M. Blenkin and A.V. Kelly

Assessment has always been a major feature of education in the early years. This book has three objectives: to identify the essential features of forms of assessment which will be genuinely supportive of education in the early years; to help teachers in their search for such forms; and to evaluate the likely impact of the system of external assessment currently being imposed.

1 85396 153 1 Paper 1992 200pp £11.95

CHILDREN AND DAY CARE

Lessons from Research

Eilis Hennessy, Sue Martin, Peter Moss and Edward Melhuish

A number of questions relevant to child development are being asked now that more children spend some of their pre-school years in day care. These questions include: Are there differences in the development of children in different types of day care? How do children in day care fare when they go to school? This book looks at these and other questions and at the research relevant to the development of these children.

1 85396 184 1 Paper 1992 128pp £9.95

PLANNING FOR EARLY LEARNING
Education in the First Five Years

Victoria Hurst

In this book for parents and practitioners the author explores what a good start for the under-fives looks like, and how it can be built into the provision we make for them.

1 85396 129 9 Paper 1991 176pp £9.95

CONTEMPORARY ISSUES IN THE EARLY YEARS
Working Collaboratively for Children

Edited by Gillian Pugh

Written against a background of major legislative change in the welfare services – education, health and social services – this book examines the key issues which present both challenges and opportunities to educators working with young children and their families in the 1990s.

1 85396 173 6 Paper 1992 176pp £9.95

THE NURSERY TEACHER IN ACTION

Margaret Lally

This book provides a detailed discussion of the responsibilities and achievements of the skilled nursery teacher.

The issues and concerns outlined are ones all nursery teachers must address in their work. The practical suggestions in the book highlight many of the ways effective nursery teachers are translating principles into practice.

1 85396 131 0 Paper 1991 208pp £9.95

EDUCATION 3–5 *SECOND EDITION*

Marion Dowling

The Second Edition of this widely used book blends a practical approach to nursery work with a consideration of research which highlights the best practices. It will be of great benefit to everyone in pre-school education.

1 85396 166 3 Paper 1992 240pp £11.95

EXPLORING LEARNING
Young Children and Blockplay

**Edited by Pat Gura with the Froebel Blockplay
Research Group directed by Tina Bruce**

This book shows how blockplay illustrates, at the
micro-level, the development of the child's
understanding of and competence in controlling
three-dimensional space.

1 85396 171 X Paper 1992 240pp £15.95

EXTENDING THOUGHT IN YOUNG CHILDREN
A Parent–Teacher Partnership

Chris Athey

This book documents invariant 'forms of thought'
used by young children, which are currently
unrecorded in the literature on children's thinking.

Throughout the book, illustrations focus on the
positive achievements of children, parents and
teachers. The book draws on a wide range of
research and advances educational theory in the
early years.

1 85396 182 6 Paper 1990 256pp £12.95

UNDERSTANDING EARLY YEARS MATHEMATICS

Derek Haylock and Anne D. Cockburn

This book is for those who teach or are preparing to teach mathematics to children in infant or primary schools and wish to have a clearer understanding of the mathematics they teach in the classroom.

1 85396 074 8 Paper 1989 138pp £9.50

LANGUAGE AND LITERACY IN THE EARLY YEARS

Marian R. Whitehead

In this book, the author examines a broad range of issues in language, literacy and learning, concentrating on the early years of education (3–8) and on the professional interests of teachers of this age range. The book aims to deepen teachers' and students' knowledge of language, literature and literacy, and of children's learning strategies.

1 85396 070 5 Paper 1990 216pp £10.95

Order through your local bookseller, or contact:
Paul Chapman Publishing
144 Liverpool Road
London N1 1LA
Tel: 071–609–5315/6;   Fax: 071–700–1057